Dedication

I dedicate this book to my wonderful children, Christopher and Sarah

Acknowledgments

I would like to thank my wonderful family, my husband Mike, and my children Christopher and Sarah for all of their support for this book and throughout the years. Thanks also to my quartet of cats, Oreo, Reeses, Piper, and Turtle for testing each piece of fabric, block, quilt top, and finished quilt.

Many thanks to my parents Mike and Carole who gave me my first sewing machine and have always supported me in pursuing my interests and dreams. To all of my quilting friends, both local and online, thank you so much for all of your inspiration, friendship, and encouragement.

I would like to thank all of my quilting friends that helped with this book by piecing and/or quilting a quilt: Paige Taylor, Garen Sherwood, Darleen Sanford, Cindy Lange, Valorie Kasten, Cindy Kaiser, Faye Jones, Dale Hernandez, Sandra Helsel, Johellen George, Yvonne Fuchs, Ruth Freyer, Delia Dorn, Cindy Clifton, Jackie Callis, Dana Blasi, Michele Blake, and Carol Alperin.

Many thanks to Andover Fabrics, Art Gallery Fabrics, United Notions / Moda Fabrics, Riley Blake Fabrics, Robert Kaufman Fabrics, Northcott / Figo Fabrics, the Warm Company, and Aurifil for their generous donations of fabric, batting, and thread.

I would like to thank the photographer, Callie, for bringing my quilts to life in photographs and to thank the family that allowed us to photograph the quilts in their beautiful houses. Last, and certainly not least, I would like to thank Yvonne Fuchs, for being amazing, supportive, and all around one of the best people I have ever met.

Contents ■

Projects ■

Introduction   6

Charm Packs 101   8

Finishing Your Quilt   124

About the Author   126

About the Quilter   127

Gift Box   20

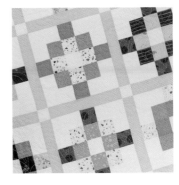

Betty   27

Lovers Lane   33

Morning Flower Patch   40

Just Two Charm Pack

two

Cheryl Brickey

SLASH YOUR STASH

Make 16 Throw Quilts

QUILTS

stash BOOKS.

an imprint of C&T Publishing

PUBLISHER: Amy Barrett-Daffin

CREATIVE DIRECTOR: Gailen Runge

SENIOR EDITOR: Roxane Cerda

TECHNICAL EDITOR: Gailen Runge

COVER/BOOK DESIGNER: April Mostek

PRODUCTION COORDINATOR: Tim Manibusan

ILLUSTRATORS: Cheryl Brickey and Aliza Shalit

PHOTOGRAPHY COORDINATOR: Rachel Ackley

PHOTOGRAPHY by Callie Whittle, unless otherwise noted

FRONT COVER PHOTOGRAPHY by Callie Whittle

Published by Stash Books, an imprint of
C&T Publishing, Inc., P.O. Box 1456, Lafayette, CA 94549

Library of Congress Cataloging-in-Publication Data

Names: Brickey, Cheryl, 1978- author.

Title: Just two charm pack quilts : slash your stash; make 16 throw quilts

/ Cheryl Brickey.

Description: Lafayette, CA : Stash Books, an imprint of C&T Publishing,

Inc., [2023] | Summary: "Included inside readers will find a mix of both

sixteen brand-new and old collection charm packs. Cheryl shows readers

ways to combine charm packs from two different collections, how to make

your own charm pack, and how you can augment a charm pack for the

perfect quilt, and more"-- Provided by publisher.

Identifiers: LCCN 2022061395 | ISBN 9781644033739 (trade paperback) | ISBN

9781644033746 (ebook)

Subjects: LCSH: Quilting--Patterns. | Patchwork--Patterns.

Classification: LCC TT835 .B69959 2023 | DDC 746.46/041--dc23/eng/20230203

LC record available at https://lccn.loc.gov/2022061395

Printed in the USA

10 9 8 7 6 5 4 3 2 1

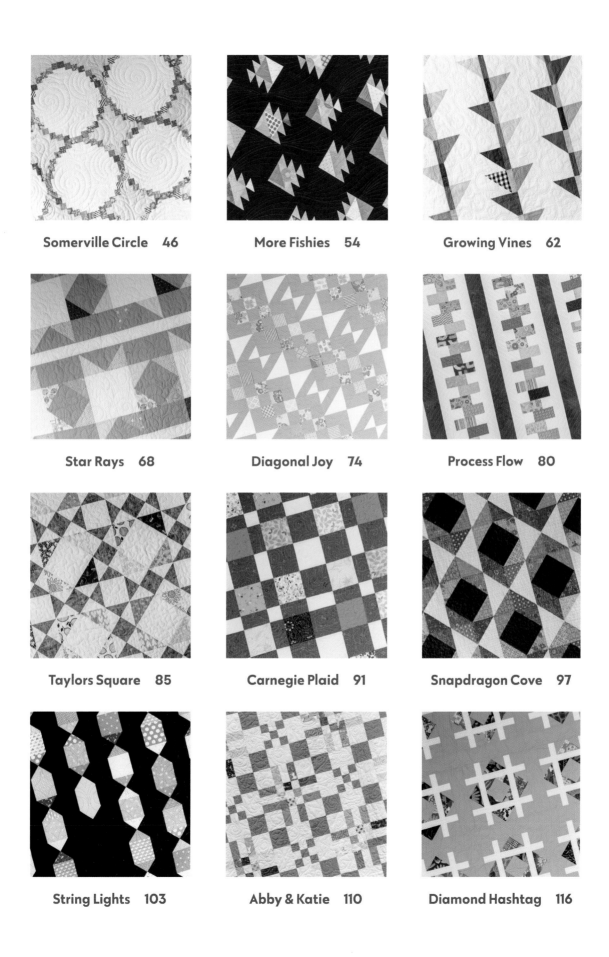

Somerville Circle   46

More Fishies   54

Growing Vines   62

Star Rays   68

Diagonal Joy   74

Process Flow   80

Taylors Square   85

Carnegie Plaid   91

Snapdragon Cove   97

String Lights   103

Abby & Katie   110

Diamond Hashtag   116

Introduction ■

Confession time, I love charm packs. When new fabric collections come out, I tend to purchase a charm pack or two as they are an inexpensive and convenient way to collect a large variety of coordinating prints. Those little packs are just too cute and seem to sneak their way into my shopping cart, both online and in my local shops.

But once you bring your charm packs home, what do you do with them? A lot of the time, because I bought them without a project in mind, the charm packs rest in my stash for months and sometimes years. While they do look pretty sitting on a shelf, it's time to put those charm packs to work and use them to create some beautiful quilts!

My first charm pack book, *Just One Charm Pack Quilts*, uses a single charm pack, an additional fabric, and a background fabric to make a quilt. The quilts in the first book were perfect for babies, kids, smaller lap quilts, and more, but I heard from many quilters that wanted to use their stash of charm packs in larger quilts.

I set out to create a book of larger quilts, perfect for adult-sized throws or lap quilts but I needed a few more charm squares. Thus, *Just Two Charm Pack Quilts* was born!

Using two charm packs, along with an additional fabric and a background fabric, I created 16 larger quilt patterns. Only have one charm pack and want to make one of the quilts from this book? No problem! I'll show you how to expand one charm into two or even how to create your own charm packs right from your stash. Let's get sewing!

Charm Packs 101 ■

Charm packs are curated collections of prints and colors created by a fabric designer or manufacturer to ensure they will work well together. Each pack typically contains between about 25 to 40 different prints, so there are usually at least a few print repeats in the pack. The charm pack usually includes a selection of prints with different scales (large and small prints), print types (florals, stripes, dots, etc.), and a variety of colors that all coordinate.

The patterns in this book assume that each charm pack contains 42 squares of 5″ × 5″ fabric, but the quantity included in charm packs varies, so be sure to compare the number of fabric pieces from your selected charm pack with the quilt pattern instructions. Different manufacturers sometimes have different names for charm packs, which are also known as 5″ Stackers, Maple Squares, Charm Rolls, or Bali Snaps.

Newer charm packs can be found in your local quilt shops and online fabric and craft stores. Try searching sites like Etsy, Ebay, and Facebook shopping groups to find older or out of print charm packs by your favorite designer or brand.

Check the Size

Charm squares are usually labeled as 5″ × 5″ square and generally have pinked edges (edges cut in a zigzag pattern to help prevent fraying). Before starting to work, check that the charm squares you have are actually 5″ × 5″ square.

For some manufacturers, the 5″ is measured between the tips of the pinked edges, while other manufacturers might measure the 5″ between the valleys of the pinked edges, as shown in the illustration, below, with exaggerated pinked edges. Prior to piecing, taking the time to measure the charm squares to know which measurement is 5″ will save a lot of frustration and time when you begin cutting and piecing blocks together.

tip CUTTING CHARM SQUARES

If the 5″ is measured between the tips of the pinked edges, be sure to align the tips of the charm square with your ruler when cutting or with another fabric when piecing. If the 5″ is measured between the valleys, for the best accuracy, it might be easiest to trim the charm squares down to a true 5″ square before using them.

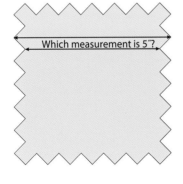

Which measurement is 5″?

Picking the Charm Pack Squares

Most charm packs contain squares of light, medium, and darker prints. Depending on the selected additional and background fabric, you may wish to leave out some of the charm squares that have a low contrast (meaning that they are similar in color) with the additional and/or background fabric. Most of the patterns in this book require between 60 and 80 charm squares so that it's possible to exclude the low contrast charm squares and still have enough left to make the project.

If you find that after removing these low contrast charm squares you do not have enough squares for the project, you can add in additional prints.

Adding in Additional Prints

If you decide to leave out a number of your charm squares and find that you don't have enough left to make the project, or you are starting with one charm pack and need 30 to 40 more charm squares, there are four easy ways to "expand" your charm packs:

1. If the charm pack is current and yardage and, or fat quarters are available from the fabric collection, you can buy an additional charm pack or additional yardage of a few chosen prints and cut the yardage into squares.

For the alternate colorway of *Diagonal Joy* (quilt project, page 74; alternate colorway fabric information, page 79), I wanted to use the remnants of a jelly roll (a precut bundle containing strips 2½″ × width of fabric) of a very old collection called Oh Deer by MoMo for Moda Fabrics. I was able to find a 10+ year old charm pack of Oh Deer listed on Etsy to have enough fabric to make the quilt.

2. If the charm pack is older and yardage is no longer available, try looking at newer fabric lines from the same designer. Many fabric designers' collections are designed to coordinate with past collections and it may work well to add in some prints from a newer fabric line.

The alternate colorway of *Star Rays* (quilt project, page 68; alternate colorway fabric information, page 73) uses a charm pack each of Elixir and Camellia, by Melody Miller for Ruby Star Society. Because both charm packs are by the same designer, the prints and colors went well together and the resultant quilt had even more print variety.

The alternate colorway of *Diagonal Joy* used one charm pack plus the scraps from a jelly roll of an older fabric collection called Oh Deer (quilt project, page 74; alternate colorway fabric information, page 79)

The alternate colorway of *Star Rays* uses two different fabric collections by the same designer which go well together (quilt project, page 68; alternate colorway fabric information, page 73)

3. Add in some solid fabrics in matching or coordinating colors. There are hundreds of solid fabric colors available, so it is not difficult to find a couple that will work with any charm pack. Solid fabrics are also prefect for the additional fabric A in the patterns.

4. Shop your stash. Look through your stash and you will most likely be pleasantly surprised to find prints that can supplement the charm pack prints you want to use.

In the main colorway of *More Fishies* (page 54), I was short about 10 squares after taking out the pink and navy prints from my Breeze by Zen Chic charm packs. I was able to shop my stash for some additional light to medium blue prints that complemented the charm prints.

I used the Woven charm pack for this version of *Cat's Eye* from *Just One Charm Pack Quilts* and felt that the gray/white prints were too close to the white background, so I excluded them. This left me with a few charm squares less than the required amount, so I added some solid charm squares from my stash in matching pink and green.

The main colorway of *More Fishies* used the Breeze fabric collection by Zen Chic for Moda Fabrics along with some additional prints I pulled from my stash after I had removed a number of charm squares (page 54)

For the main colorway of *Lovers Lane* (page 33), I wanted to make the quilt using a charm pack of Clementine (which I used in *Circus Stars* from *Just One Charm Pack Quilts*), but I only had one charm pack and was not able to find another for sale so I shopped my stash to expand the one charm pack into two.

The main colorway of *Lovers Lane* used a single charm pack along with various prints in coordinating colors from my stash (page 33)

tip EXPANDING ONE CHARM PACK TO TWO

When I add in fabrics from my stash to build my one charm pack into two, I tend to pull out all of the fabrics I have that might work with the colors and prints of the charm pack (which does make a little mess). I then look at all of the fabrics and narrow my section down, making sure to have a good variety of different types of prints. I find it easier to start with a large number of fabrics and then cut the number down versus having to go back to my stash to add in more fabrics. You do not have to match the colors of the stash squares to the charm square exactly, having a little difference adds interest to the quilt top.

Make Your Own Charm Pack

You don't need to start with premade charm packs to make these quilts, you can create your own charm pack!

From Color Inspiration

1. Pick a color scheme. You can build your charm packs by picking out one or two colors. You can use your favorite colors, like I did with the navy blue prints in the alternate colorway of *More Fishies* (quilt project page 54; alternate colorway fabric information, page 61) or in the main colorway of *Somerville Circle* (page 46) where I used all red prints from Bonnie and Camille. You could also create packs using all of the same type of print such as all plaids or all polka dots.

Navy blue was the inspiration for this alternate version of *More Fishies* (quilt project page 54; alternate colorway fabric information, page 61)

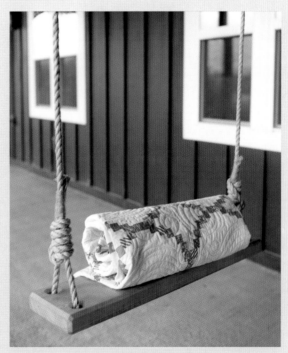

The main colorway of *Somerville Circle* used red prints from many different Bonnie and Camille fabric collections (page 46)

2. Pick a color palette inspiration. Another way to come up with a color scheme is to find a fabric print (or picture) you like and then use that to pick fabrics. For the alternate colorway of *Betty*, I started with a favorite Bonnie and Camille print and pulled matching red, aqua, and pink prints to match and coordinate.

Starting with a focal fabric, I pulled prints, blenders, and solids that are similar to the focal fabric colors. The additional fabric colors do not need to match exactly; having slight color variations gives the quilt interest. Once I have a large number of fabrics pulled from my stash, I narrow down my selection of fabrics, while trying to maintain a good mix of colors, scale of prints, types of print, and solids. I suggest cutting no more than 2–5 squares 5″ × 5″ of each fabric for the custom charm packs. You can use your inspiration fabric in the quilt top as one of the fabrics or even use it in the backing or binding.

The alternate colorway of *Betty* used a variety of Bonnie and Camille prints from various fabric lines. I started with one print and pulled coordinating fabrics from there (quilt project, page 27; alternate colorway fabric information, page 32)

tip SELVEDGE COLORS
If you are unsure which colors are in a fabric print, usually the selvedge has color spots to aid in color matching.

From other Pre-cuts and Yardage

Do you have lots of scraps, fat quarters, or other yardage?

I like to cut my fabric scraps from other projects into 5″ × 5″ pieces and store them together. I also add in unused extra charm squares from other quilt projects. You can "shop" this stack of charm squares to create your next quilt.

Many of the quilts in this book were made from layer cakes (10″ × 10″ pieces) and fat quarter bundles due to the pre-cuts that the fabric manufacturers had on hand.

To cut charm squares from other pre-cuts and yardage:

Pre-cut or yardage	# of charm squares per piece
10″ × 10″ pre-cuts (called layer cakes, or 10″ stackers)	4
Fat quarters (at least 18″ × 20″)	12
½ yard	24

The Supporting Fabrics

The background, additional fabric (fabric A), and binding fabrics can be selected to compliment the charm prints and the design of the quilt.

Background Fabric

The background fabric, in many cases, forms a good amount of the quilt top and can impact the way the quilt looks. Picking a background fabric that has good contrast with the charm squares is key to have the piecing and quilt design stand out.

I tend to pick a solid print or a tone-on-tone or subtle print, that reads like a solid from a distance, for my backgrounds. If a large-scale floral or a bright gingham print were used as the background, it may be more difficult to see the quilt design and shapes created by the charm squares.

For *String Lights* (page 103), the main colorway is made with a black background and the alternate colorway has a white background. You can see from these quilts, how different the finished quilt can look by switching out the background color.

tip MY FAVORITE BACKGROUND FABRICS

My favorite background fabrics to use are white, cream, gray, or black solids. Solids allow the piecing and prints to shine and be the focus and solids also have the added benefit of usually being cheaper than print fabrics.

The different background colors in the two versions of *String Lights* (page 103) give the quilts completely different looks.

Additional Fabric (Fabric A in the Patterns)

Each of the patterns in the book utilizes an additional fabric (fabric A) in addition to the charm squares and background fabric. This additional fabric helps "stretch" the charm packs enough to make a full quilt and is usually a color and, or a print that has enough contrast with both the charm pack fabrics and the background fabric.

To choose the additional fabric, look at the pattern to see if the additional fabric touches the charm squares and/or background fabric. In *Gift Box* (page 20), the additional fabric, the background fabric, and the charm squares are all right next to each other so the pattern looks best when there is good contrast between all of them. On the other hand, in *Diagonal Joy* (page 74), the additional fabric is only next to the background fabric (it does not touch any of the charm square) so there is less worry about the contrast between the additional fabric and the charm squares.

Most of the quilts in the book use solid fabrics or tone-on-tone blenders as the additional fabric, but for a different look, the additional fabric can be a bold choice. In the main colorway of *Growing Vines* (page 62), the charm packs are solids and the additional fabric is a fun gingham print.

One of the prints from the charm pack might work well as the additional fabric, but if your charm pack has been aging like fine wine in your sewing room and the prints from the collection are no longer available, a solid fabric is a great choice. There are so many solid fabric colors available that there is sure to be a color that works well with the charm squares and background fabric.

The main colorway of *Growing Vines* (page 62) with solid fabrics as the charm squares and a gingham print as the additional fabric

Binding Fabrics

The most popular way to finish a quilt is with binding. Binding is a strip of fabric that wraps around and encloses the raw edges of the quilt top. For instructions on how to bind a quilt, see Binding (page 124).

Selecting fabric for the binding is a personal preference. I view binding as a frame for the quilt, so I tend to use a binding that is darker than most the quilt, like in the alternate colorway of *Snapdragon Cove* (quilt project, page 97; alternate colorway fabric information, page 102). Another option for binding fabric is to use one of the prints from the charm pack, such as in the main colorway of *Snapdragon Cove* (quilt project, page 97). I would only caution against using a white or very light binding fabric for a baby or child's quilt as these may show dirt more easily.

The binding of the main colorway of *Snapdragon Cove* (quilt project, page 97) uses a print from the charm pack as the binding.

The binding of the alternate colorway of *Snapdragon Cove* (quilt project, page 97; alternate colorway fabric information, page 102) uses a dark fabric as the binding.

For most quilts, I do not decide what binding to use until the quilt has been quilted and the batting has been trimmed. Often, the binding I have in mind when I start the quilt does not wind up being my final pick once the quilt is quilted. To audition different fabrics as potential binding fabrics, I place several different fabrics under the edge of the quilt so that they peek out about ½˝ from the quilt top to mimic what they would look like as a binding. For example, I had originally planned to use the same gingham print as the additional fabric for the main colorway of *Growing Vines* (page 62), but once I auditioned fabrics after the quilt was quilted, I thought the gingham was too busy and went with a solid brown instead.

For the main colorway of *Growing Vines*, (page 62) I originally was planning on using the same gingham as the additional fabric, but after auditioning fabrics I choose a less busy solid.

tip STRAIGHT GRAIN VERSUS BIAS GRAIN BINDING

The instructions and fabric requirements for the quilts in this book are for straight grain binding, meaning that the strips for the binding are cut from selvage to selvage. Some quilters prefer a bias binding where the strips are cut at a 45° angle to the selvages. If bias binding is your preferred method for binding, additional binding fabric may be required compared to what is listed in the pattern.

Gift Box

Pieced by Jackie Callis and quilted by Carol Alperin

finished block
16˝ × 16˝

finished quilt
58½˝ × 76˝

social media
#GiftBoxQuilt

FABRIC FROM THE ATTIC is one of my all-time favorite fabric collections; there is such a variety of colors used in the fabrics that I would never have thought to put together, but they work so well as a whole collection.

Gift Box is a fun quilt design to piece together because the secondary pattern emerges as the blocks and sashing are sewn together.

FABRICS USED

- **Charm Packs:** *Fabric from the Attic by Giucy Giuce for Andover Fabrics*
- **Fabric A:** *Century Solids in Smoke by Andover Fabrics Canvas*
- **Background fabric:** *Century Solids in Snow by Andover Fabrics Canvas*

Fabric Requirements

Width of fabrics (WOF) is assumed to be at least 40˝.

CHARM SQUARES 5˝ × 5˝: 72

FABRIC A (WHITE): 1 yard

BACKGROUND (BG) FABRIC (GRAY): 2⅞ yards

BINDING: ⅝ yard

BACKING FABRIC: 4⅔ yards

BATTING: 67˝ × 84˝

Cutting Instructions

CHARM SQUARES

No cutting required, charm squares will be used as 5˝ × 5˝ pieces.

FABRIC A (WHITE)

- Cut 6 strips 4½˝ × WOF.
  a. Sub-cut the strips into 48 squares 4½˝ × 4½˝ (each strip can yield 8 squares).

- Cut 1 strip 2˝ × WOF.
  a. Sub-cut the strip into 20 cornerstones 2˝ × 2˝.

BACKGROUND (BG) FABRIC (GRAY)

- Cut 2 strips 6¼˝ × WOF.
  a. Sub-cut the strips into 12 squares 6¼˝ × 6¼˝ (each strip can yield 6 squares).

- Cut 6 strips 5˝ × WOF.
  a. Sub-cut the strips into 48 squares 5˝ × 5˝ (each strip can yield 8 squares).

- Cut 7 strips 2½˝ × WOF for the border.

- Cut 16 strips 2˝ × WOF.
  a. Sub-cut the strips into 31 rectangles 2˝ × 16½˝ (each strip can yield 2 rectangles).

BINDING FABRIC

Cut 7 strips 2½˝ × WOF.

Piecing the Blocks

A scant ¼˝ (a thread width smaller than ¼˝) seam is to be used throughout the construction of the quilt top unless otherwise instructed.

Half-Square Triangle (HST) Units

1. Place a charm square 5˝ × 5˝ and a bg square 5˝ × 5˝ right sides together. Draw a diagonal line using a removable marking device on the back of the lighter square (shown as the solid line).

2. Sew a ¼˝ seam on both sides of the solid line (shown as the dotted lines). Cut on the solid line and press the seam open or towards the darker fabric.

3. Trim the HST units to 4½˝ × 4½˝. Note: each set of one charm square and one bg square will yield two HST units.

4. Repeat steps 1–3 to make a total of 96 HST units 4½˝ × 4½˝. You will use 48 of the charm squares.

 =

Doublet Units

1. Sew together 2 HST units 4½″ × 4½″, pressing the seam open, to make a doublet unit 4½″ × 8½″.

2. Repeat to make a total of 48 doublet units.

Square in a Square (SiaS) Units

Use a variety of prints within each square in a square unit.

1. Cut the remaining 24 charm squares 5″ × 5″ each in half once on the diagonal to make a total of 48 triangles 5″ × 5″.

2. Center a charm triangle 5″ × 5″ along a first side of a bg square 6¼″ × 6¼″. Sew along the edge (seam shown as a dotted line), pressing the seam open or outwards.

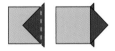

3. Sew a second charm triangle 5″ × 5″ on the side of the bg square opposite to the first side, pressing the seam open or outwards. Both of these triangles can be sewn on and then pressed instead of pressing after each addition.

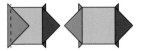

3. Continue by sewing 2 charm triangles 5″ × 5″ onto the other 2 sides of the square, pressing seams open or outwards.

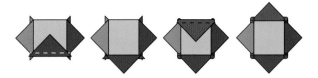

4. Trim off the tabs (dog ears) formed by the sewn on triangles and square the unit to 8½″ × 8½″ (if necessary) making sure there is ¼″ between the corner of the inner square and the outer side of the unit.

5. Repeat steps 2–5 to make a total of 12 square in a square (SiaS) units 8½″ × 8½″.

Block Assembly

1. Arrange the following units and pieces according to the diagram:

    1 SiaS unit 8½″ × 8½″

    4 doublet units 4½″ × 8½″

    4 fabric A squares 4½″ × 4½″

2. Sew the units and pieces into rows, pressing the seams open or towards the doublet units.

3. Sew the rows together, pressing seams open, to make a block 16½″ × 16½″ (16″ × 16″ finished in the quilt top).

4. Repeat to make a total of 12 blocks.

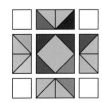

Quilt Top Assembly

Block Rows

1. Sew together the following blocks and sashing pieces, pressing the seams open or towards the sashing pieces, to make a block row 16½˝ × 54½˝.

> 3 blocks 16½˝ × 16½˝
>
> 4 bg rectangles 2˝ × 16½˝

2. Repeat to make a total of 4 block rows.

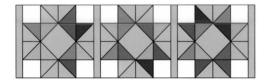

Sashing Rows

1. Sew together the following pieces, pressing the seams open or towards the sashing pieces to make a sashing row 2˝ × 54½˝.

> 3 bg rectangles 2˝ × 16½˝
>
> 4 cornerstone squares 2˝ × 2˝

2. Repeat to make a total of 5 sashing rows.

Putting Them Together

Sew together the following rows as shown in the quilt top assembly diagram below, pressing the seams open, to make the quilt top.

> 4 block rows 16½˝ × 54½˝
>
> 5 sashing rows 2˝ × 54½˝

The quilt top, before borders are added, should measure 54½˝ × 72˝.

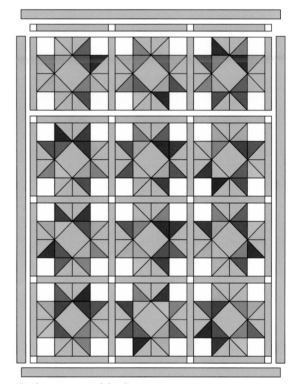

Quilt top assembly diagram

Border

Refer to the quilt top assembly diagram.

1. Sew together 2 bg strips 2½″ × WOF and trim to the average height of the quilt, approx. 72″. Repeat to make a second border.

2. Sew borders onto the sides of the quilt top, pressing the seams open or towards the borders.

3. Cut 1 bg strip 2½″ × WOF in half and sew each half to a full bg strip 2½″ × WOF. Trim to the average width of the quilt, approx. 58½″.

4. Sew borders onto the top and bottom of the quilt top, pressing seams open or towards the borders.

The finished quilt top should measure approx. 58½″ × 76″.

Finishing

Refer to Finishing the Quilt (page 124) for instructions on how to finish the quilt.

1. Make the quilt backing:

Remove selvages, cut into 2 pieces (about 84″ × WOF) and sew backing pieces together along the trimmed selvage edges using a ½″ seam, pressing the seam open. Trim to approx. 67″ × 84″. *Note that the seam will be vertical in the backing.*

2. Layer the quilt top, batting, and backing. Baste and quilt as desired. The main colorway of the *Gift Box* quilt was quilted with a filled orange peel design.

3. Trim off selvages from the binding strips 2½" × WOF and sew together end-to-end to make the binding. Bind and enjoy your quilt!

alternate colorway

Pieced by Cheryl Brickey and quilted by Bear Creek Quilting Company

FABRICS USED

- **Charm Packs:** *Cozy & Magical* and *Plaid of My Dreams* by Maureen Cracknell for Art Gallery Fabrics
- **Fabric A:** *Pure Solids in Ash by Art Gallery Fabrics*
- **Background fabric:** *Pure Solids in White Linen Grunge by Art Gallery Fabrics*

I love the holiday and plaid collections from Maureen Cracknell which incorporate some non-traditional holiday colors. I used a combination of the two collections for extra print variety and because they coordinate so well. The alternate colorway of *Gift Box* quilt was quilted with a modern snowflake design.

Betty

Pieced and quilted by
Cheryl Brickey

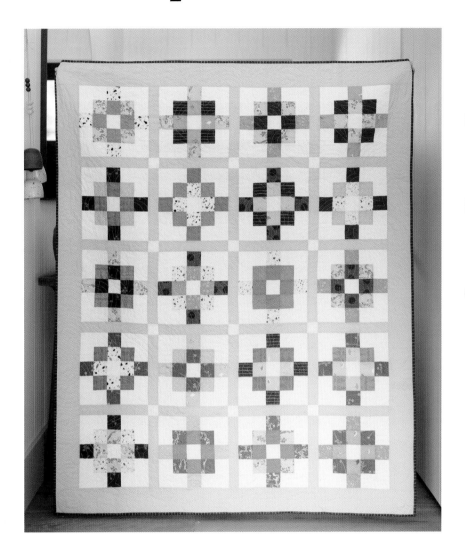

finished block
10″ × 10″

finished quilt
52″ × 63½″

social media

#BettyQuilt

THE BLOCKS IN THIS QUILT reminded me of crocheted granny square blocks so I named this quilt Betty after my grandmother. I love how each block looks different based on the where the darker and lighter prints are placed.

Fabric Requirements

Width of fabrics (WOF) is assumed to be at least 40˝.

CHARM SQUARES 5˝ × 5˝: 60

FABRIC A (WHITE): 1⅜ yards

BACKGROUND (BG) FABRIC (PEACH): 1½ yards

BINDING: ½ yard

BACKING FABRIC: 3⅓ yards

BATTING: 60˝ × 72˝

Cutting Instructions

CHARM SQUARES

The charm squares 5˝ × 5˝ will be cut during the piecing instructions.

FABRIC A (WHITE)

- Cut 17 strips 2½˝ × WOF.

  a. Sub-cut 10 strips into 80 rectangles 2½˝ × 4½˝ (each strip can yield 8 rectangles).

  b. Sub-cut 7 strips into 100 squares 2½˝ × 2½˝ (each strip can yield 16 squares).

- Cut 1 strip 2˝ × WOF.

  a. Sub-cut the strip into 12 cornerstones 2˝ × 2˝.

BACKGROUND (BG) FABRIC (PEACH)

- Cut 6 strips 4˝ × WOF for the border.

- Cut 11 strips 2˝ × WOF.

  a. Sub-cut the strips into 31 sashing pieces 2˝ × 10½˝ (each strip can yield 3 sashing pieces).

Note: If your WOF is at least 42˝, then you can cut 4 sashing pieces from each WOF and will only need 8 strips.

BINDING FABRIC

Cut 6 strips 2½˝ × WOF.

Piecing Instructions

A scant ¼˝ (a thread width smaller than ¼˝) seam is to be used throughout the construction of the quilt top unless otherwise instructed.

Block Assembly

1. Select 3 charm squares (with different colors and/or prints) to be used in one block. Cut each charm square in half once horizontally and vertically to make 4 matching squares 2½˝ × 2½˝.

tip EASIER GROUPING

I suggest sorting the charm squares into groups of 3 for all 20 blocks before cutting to ensure a good mix of prints within each block.

2. Sew together the following pieces, pressing all seams open or following the arrows, to make a block 10½″ × 10½″.

- 4 matching squares 2½″ × 2½″ from the first charm square
- 4 matching squares 2½″ × 2½″ from the second charm square
- 4 matching squares 2½″ × 2½″ from the third charm square
- 4 bg rectangles 2½″ × 4½″
- 5 bg squares 2½″ × 2½″

3. Repeat steps 1–2 to make a total of 20 blocks.

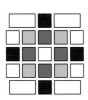 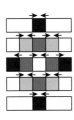

Quilt Top Assembly

Block Rows

1. Sew together the following blocks and sashing pieces, pressing the seams open or towards the sashing pieces to make a block row 10½″ × 45″.

- 4 blocks 10½″ × 10½″
- 3 sashing pieces 2″ × 10½″

2. Repeat to make a total of 5 block rows.

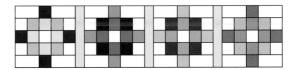

Sashing Rows

1. Sew together the following pieces, pressing the seams open or towards the sashing pieces to make a sashing row 2″ × 45″.

- 4 sashing pieces 2″ × 10½″
- 3 cornerstone squares 2″ × 2″

2. Repeat to make a total of 4 sashing rows.

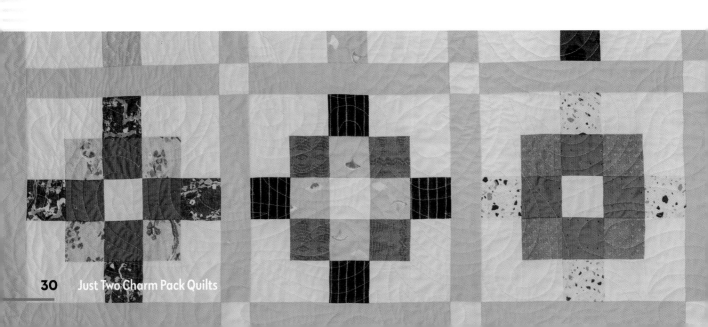

Quilt Top Assembly

Sew together the following rows as shown in the quilt top assembly diagram, pressing the seams open, to make the quilt top.

5 block rows 10½˝ × 45˝

4 sashing rows 2˝ × 45˝

The quilt top, before borders are added, should measure 45˝ × 56½˝.

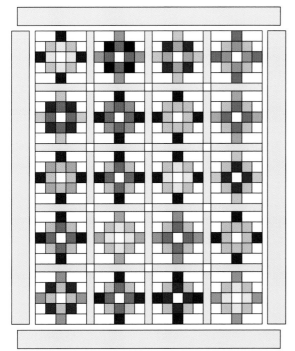

Quilt top assembly diagram

Border

Refer to the quilt top assembly diagram.

1. Cut 1 bg strip 4˝ × WOF in half and sew each half to a full bg strip 4˝ × WOF. Trim to the average height of the quilt, approx. 56½˝.

2. Sew borders onto the sides of the quilt top, pressing the seams open or towards the borders.

3. Cut 1 bg strip 4˝ × WOF in half and sew each half to a full bg strip 4˝ × WOF. Trim to the average width of the quilt, approx. 52˝.

4. Sew borders onto the top and bottom of the quilt top, pressing seams open or towards the borders.

The finished quilt top should measure approx. 52˝ × 63½˝.

Finishing

Refer to Finishing the Quilt (page 124) for instructions on how to finish the quilt.

1. Make the quilt backing:

Remove selvages, cut into 2 pieces (about 60˝ × WOF) and sew backing pieces together along the trimmed selvage edges using a ½˝ seam, pressing the seam open. Trim to approx. 60˝ × 72˝.

2. Layer the quilt top, batting, and backing. Baste and quilt as desired. The main colorway of *Betty* quilt was quilted with a large paisley design.

3. Trim off selvages from the binding strips 2½˝ × WOF and sew together end-to-end to make the binding. Bind and enjoy your quilt!

alternate colorway

Pieced and quilted by Valorie Kasten

FABRICS USED

- **Charm Packs:** *Various red, pink, and aqua prints by Bonnie and Camille for Moda Fabrics*
- **Fabric A:** *Bella Solids in White by Moda Fabrics*
- **Background fabric:** *Bella Solids in Zen Gray by Moda Fabrics*

Valorie used the red, pink, and aqua prints in the same positions within each block, instead of a more random arrangement, which results in a quilt that is cohesive and yet still scrappy. The alternate colorway of the *Betty* quilt was quilted with a modern Baptist fan-like design.

Lovers Lane

Pieced by Cheryl Brickey and quilted by Bear Creek Quilting Company

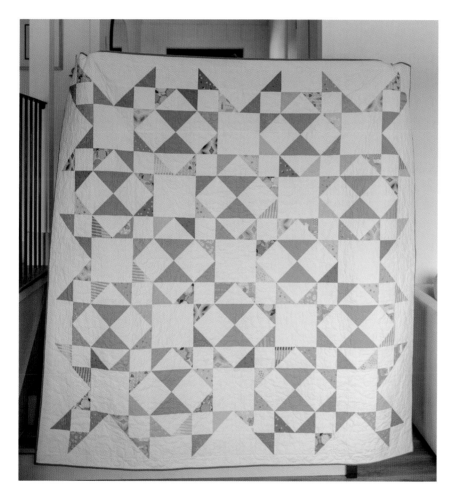

finished block
8″ × 16″

finished quilt
76½″ × 76½″

social media
#LoversLaneQuilt

I HAD ONE CHARM PACK of Clementine left over from my previous book, *Just One Charm Pack Quilts* (Circus Stars, alternate colorway on page 66) and really wanted to use it in the *Lovers Lane* quilt. I was not able to purchase another charm pack of this older collection so I "expanded" the one charm pack into two by using the techniques in Adding in Additional Prints (page 9).

Fabric Requirements

Width of fabrics (WOF) is assumed to be at least 40˝.

CHARM SQUARES 5˝ × 5˝: 72

FABRIC A (RED): ⅝ yard

BACKGROUND (BG) FABRIC (WHITE): 4⅝ yards

BINDING: ¾ yard

BACKING FABRIC: 7⅛ yards

BATTING: 85˝ × 85˝

Cutting Instructions

CHARM SQUARES

The charm squares 5˝ × 5˝ will be used without further cutting.

FABRIC A (RED)

- Cut 2 strips 9½˝ × WOF.

  a. Sub-cut the strips into 6 squares 9½˝ × 9½˝ (each strip can yield 4 squares).

BACKGROUND (BG) FABRIC (WHITE)

- Cut 2 strips 9½˝ × WOF.

  a. Sub-cut 1 strip into 4 squares 9½˝ × 9½˝.

  b. Sub-cut 1 strip into 2 squares 9½˝ × 9½˝ and 1 square 8½˝ × 8½˝.

- Cut 3 strips 8½˝ × WOF.

  a. Sub-cut the strips into 12 squares 8½˝ × 8½˝ (each strip can yield 4 squares).

- Cut 9 strips 5˝ × WOF.

  a. Sub-cut the strips into 72 squares 5˝ × 5˝ (each strip can yield 8 squares).

- Cut 10 strips 4½˝ × WOF.

  a. Sub-cut 5 strips into 20 rectangles 4½˝ × 8½˝ (each strip can yield 4 rectangles).

  b. Sub-cut 5 strips into 40 squares 4½˝ × 4½˝ (each strip can yield 8 squares).

- Cut 8 strips 2½˝ × WOF for the border.

BINDING FABRIC

Cut 8 strips 2½˝ × WOF.

Piecing Instructions

A scant ¼˝ (a thread width smaller than ¼˝) seam is to be used throughout the construction of the quilt top unless otherwise instructed.

Half-Square Triangle (HST) Units

1. Place a charm square 5˝ × 5˝ and a bg square 5˝ × 5˝ right sides together. Draw a diagonal line using a removable marking device on the back of the lighter square (shown as the solid line).

2. Sew a ¼˝ seam on both sides of the solid line (shown as the dotted lines). Cut on the solid line and press the seam open or towards the darker fabric.

3. Trim the HST units to 4½˝ × 4½˝. Note: each set of one charm square and one bg square will yield two HST units.

4. Repeat steps 1–3 to make a total of 144 HST units 4½˝ × 4½˝.

 =

FABRICS USED

- **Charm Packs:** *1 charm pack of Clementine by Melody Miller from Ruby Star Society for Moda Fabrics plus scraps*

- **Fabric A:** *Moda Bella Solids in Geranium*

- **Background fabric:** *Moda Bella Solids in White*

Hourglass Units

1. Place a fabric A square 9½″ × 9½″ and a bg fabric square 9½″ × 9½″ right sides together. Draw a diagonal line using a removable marking device on the back of the lighter square (shown as the solid line).

2. Sew a ¼″ seam on both sides of the solid line (shown as the dotted lines). Cut on the solid line and press the seam towards the darker fabric. *Do not trim these HST units.*

3. Repeat steps 1–2 to make a total of 12 HST units. *fig A*

4. Place two HST units (about 9″ × 9″) right sides together such that the seams nest together and HST units are oriented as shown in the illustration.

5. Draw a diagonal line using a removable marking device on the back of the one of the HST units (shown as the solid line) perpendicular to the seam of that HST unit.

6. Sew a ¼″ seam on each side of the solid line (shown as the dotted lines). Cut on the solid line, press seams open, and trim hourglass units to 8½″ × 8½″.

7. Repeat steps 3–5 to make a total of 12 hourglass units 8½″ × 8½″. *fig B*

Doublet Units

1. Sew together 2 HST units 4½″ × 4½″, pressing the seam open, to make a doublet unit 4½″ × 8½″.

2. Repeat to make a total of 60 doublet units 4½″ × 8½″. *Note: There will be 24 HST units left over. fig C*

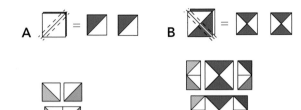

Block Assembly

1. Sew together the following units, pressing the seams open, to make a block 8½″ × 16½″.

  1 hourglass unit 8½″ × 8½″

  2 doublet units 4½″ × 8½″

2. Repeat to make a total of 12 blocks 8½″ × 16½″. *fig D*

Quilt Top Assembly

It is recommended that all seams are pressed open during the quilt top assembly unless otherwise noted.

First Rows

1. Sew together the following blocks, units, and pieces to make a first row 8½″ × 72½″.

  2 blocks 8½″ × 16½″

  2 doublet units 4½″ × 8½″

  3 bg squares 8½″ × 8½″

  2 bg rectangles 4½″ × 8½″

2. Repeat to make a total of 3 first rows. *fig E*

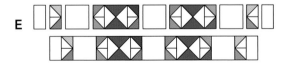

Second Rows

1. Sew together the following blocks and pieces, to make a second row 8½″ × 72½″.

    3 blocks 8½″ × 16½″

    2 bg squares 8½″ × 8½″

    2 bg rectangles 4½″ × 8½″

2. Repeat to make a total of 2 second rows.

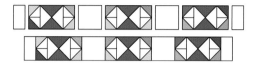

Third Rows

1. Sew together the following units and pieces to make a third row 4½″ × 72½″.

    5 doublet units 4½″ × 8½″

    2 HST units 4½″ × 4½″

    6 bg squares 4½″ × 4½″

Be sure to match the direction of all of the HST units.

2. Repeat to make a total of 6 third rows.

Fourth Rows

1. Sew together the following units and pieces to make a fourth row 4½″ × 72½″.

    6 HST units 4½″ × 4½″

    5 bg rectangles 4½″ × 8½″

    2 bg squares 4½″ × 4½″

Be sure to match the direction of all of the HST units.

2. Repeat to make a total of 2 fourth rows.

Quilt Top Assembly

Sew together the following rows as shown in the quilt top assembly diagram to make the quilt top. *Note that some rows will be rotated 180 degrees to match the diagram.*

    3 first rows 8½″ × 72½″

    2 second rows 8½″ × 72½″

    6 third rows 4½″ × 72½″

    2 fourth rows 4½″ × 72½″

The quilt top, before the borders are added, should measure 72½″ × 72½″.

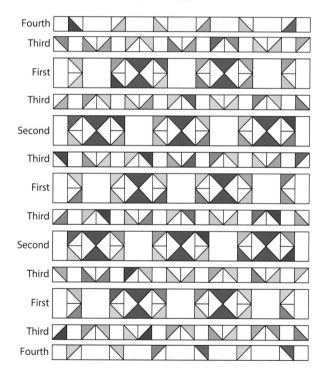

tip **EASIER ASSEMBLY**

The quilt has 13 rows, so it is helpful to label each row before sewing them together. Also, sewing the thinner rows (third and fourth) to the wider rows (first and second) first, makes sewing the quilt top together easier.

Border

Refer to the Borders Assembly Diagram.

1. Sew together 2 bg strips 2½˝ × WOF and trim to the average height of the quilt, approx. 72½˝. Repeat to make a second border.

2. Sew borders onto the sides of the quilt top, pressing seams open or towards the borders.

3. Sew together 2 bg strips 2½˝ × WOF and trim to the average width of the quilt, approx. 76½˝. Repeat to make a second border.

4. Sew borders onto the top and bottom of the quilt top, pressing seams open or towards the borders.

The finished quilt top should measure approx. 76½˝ × 76½˝.

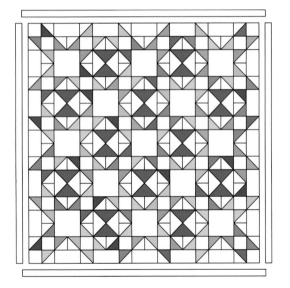

Finishing

Refer to Finishing the Quilt (page 124) for instructions on how to finish the quilt.

1. Make the quilt backing:

Remove selvages, cut into 3 pieces (about 85˝ × WOF) and sew backing pieces together along the trimmed selvage edges using a ½˝ seam, pressing the seam open. Trim to approx. 85˝ × 85˝.

2. Layer the quilt top, batting, and backing. Baste and quilt as desired. The main colorway of the *Lovers Lane* quilt was quilted with a floral swirl design.

3. Trim off selvages from the binding strips 2½˝ × WOF and sew together end-to-end to make the binding. Bind and enjoy your quilt!

alternate colorway

Pieced by Sandra Helsel and quilted by Johellen George

FABRICS USED

- **Charm Packs:** *Handstitched by Karen Lewis for Figo Fabrics*
- **Fabric A:** *Colorworks Solids in Navy by Northcott Fabrics*
- **Background fabric:** *Colorworks Solids in Smoke by Northcott Fabrics*

For a different look to the quilt top, the hourglass units in the second rows can be rotated 90 degrees (so they look more like bow ties) like in the alternate colorway. The alternate colorway of *Lovers Lane* quilt was quilted with a floral design.

Morning Flower Patch

Pieced by Dana Blasi and Cheryl Brickey and quilted by Bear Creek Quilting Company

finished block
6″ × 6″

finished quilt
58½″ × 70½″

social media
#MorningFlower
PatchQulit

MORNING FLOWER PATCH is a fun combination of a classic nine-patch block with a plus sign block. Because the charm squares are cut into 2½″ × 2½″ squares, you could also use smaller scraps or part of a jelly roll for this quilt.

FABRICS USED

- **Charm Packs:** *Enchanted Meadow by Beverly McCullough for Riley Blake Fabrics*
- **Fabric A:** *Confetti Cotton in White by Riley Blake*
- **Background fabric:** *Confetti Cotton in Charcoal by Riley Blake*

Fabric Requirements

Width of fabrics (WOF) is assumed to be at least 40˝.

CHARM SQUARES 5˝ × 5˝: 50

FABRIC A (WHITE): ⅝ yard

BACKGROUND (BG) FABRIC (GRAY): 3¼ yards

BINDING: ⅝ yard

BACKING FABRIC: 3¾ yards

BATTING: 67˝ × 79˝

Cutting Instructions

CHARM SQUARES

Cut each of the charm squares into 4 squares 2½˝ × 2½˝ for a total of 200 squares 2½˝ × 2½˝.

Note: You could instead use scraps or jelly roll strips for the 2½˝ × 2½˝ squares.

FABRIC A (WHITE)

- Cut 11 strips 1½˝ × WOF.

  a. Sub-cut 6 strips into 31 rectangles 1½˝ × 6½˝ (each strip can yield 6 rectangles).

  b. Reserve the remaining 5 strips.

BACKGROUND (BG) FABRIC (GRAY)

- Cut 3 strips 6½˝ × WOF.

  a. Sub-cut the strips into 18 squares 6½˝ × 6½˝ (each strip can yield 6 squares).

- Cut 10 strips 3˝ × WOF.

- Cut 23 strips 2½˝ × WOF.

  a. Sub-cut 16 strips into 250 squares 2½˝ × 2½˝ (each strip can yield 16 squares).

  b. Reserve the remaining 7 strips (border).

BINDING FABRIC

Cut 7 strips 2½˝ × WOF.

Piecing Instructions

A scant ¼˝ (a thread width smaller than ¼˝) seam is to be used throughout the construction of the quilt top unless otherwise instructed.

Nine-Patch Blocks

1. Using a variety of print squares within each block, arrange the following pieces as shown.

    4 charm squares 2½˝ × 2½˝

    5 bg squares 2½˝ × 2½˝

2. Sew the pieces into rows, pressing the seams away from the print squares. Sew the rows together, pressing the seams open, to make a nine patch block 6½˝ × 6½˝.

3. Repeat steps 1–2 to make a total of 50 nine patch blocks 6½˝ × 6½˝.

Plus Blocks

1. Sew together the following strips (in order) along their long sides to make a strip set 6½″ × WOF. Press the seams open or towards the darker fabric.

  1 bg strip 3″ × WOF

  1 fabric A strip 1½″ × WOF

  1 bg strip 3″ × WOF

2. Repeat to make a total of 5 strip sets.

3. Cut the strip sets into 62 units 3″ × 6½″ (each first strip set can yield 13 units).

4. Sew together 2 units 3″ × 6½″ from step 3 and 1 fabric A rectangle 1½″ × 6½″, pressing the seams open or towards the fabric A rectangle, to make a plus block 6½″ × 6½″.

5. Repeat to make a total of 31 plus blocks 6½″ × 6½″.

Plain Blocks

The 18 bg squares 6½″ × 6½″ will be used as the plain blocks 6½″ × 6½″.

Quilt Top Assembly

During the row assemblies, press all seams open or away from the nine patch blocks.

Row A

1. Sew together the following blocks to make a row A 6½″ × 54½″.

  5 nine patch blocks 6½″ × 6½″

  4 plain blocks 6½″ × 6½″

2. Repeat to make a total of 2 row A.

Row B

1. Sew together the following blocks to make a row B 6½″ × 54½″.

  4 nine patch blocks 6½″ × 6½″

  3 plus sign blocks 6½″ × 6½″

  2 plain blocks 6½″ × 6½″

2. Repeat to make a total of 5 row B.

Row C

1. Sew together the following blocks to make a row C 6½″ × 54½″.

  5 nine patch blocks 6½″ × 6½″

  4 plus blocks 6½″ × 6½″

2. Repeat to make a total of 4 row C.

Quilt Top Assembly

Sew together the 2 row A, 5 row B, and 4 row C according to the quilt top assembly diagram, pressing the seams open, to make the quilt top.

The quilt top (before the border is added) should measure 54½˝ × 66½˝.

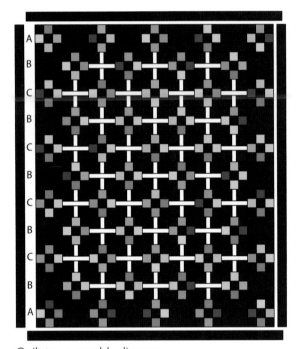

Quilt top assembly diagram

Border

Refer to the Quilt Top Assembly Diagram.

1. Sew together 2 bg strips 2½˝ × WOF and trim to the average height of the quilt, approx. 66½˝. Repeat to make a second side border.

2. Sew side borders onto the quilt top, pressing seams open or towards the borders.

3. Cut 1 bg strip 2½˝ × WOF in half and sew each half to a full bg strip 2½˝ × WOF. Trim to the average width of the quilt, approx. 58½˝.

4. Sew borders onto the top and bottom of the quilt top, pressing seams open or towards the borders.

The finished quilt top should measure approx. 58½˝ × 70½˝.

Finishing

Refer to Finishing the Quilt (page 124) for instructions on how to finish the quilt.

1. Make the quilt backing:

Remove selvages, cut into 2 pieces (about 67˝ × WOF) and sew backing pieces together along the trimmed selvage edges using a ½˝ seam, pressing the seam open. Trim to approx. 67˝ × 79˝.

2. Layer the quilt top, batting, and backing. Baste and quilt as desired. The main colorway of Morning Flower Patch quilt was quilted with a swirling vine design.

3. Trim off selvages from the binding strips 2½" × WOF and sew together end-to-end to make the binding. Bind and enjoy your quilt!

alternate colorway

Pieced by Cheryl Brickey and quilted by Johellen George

FABRICS USED

- **Charm Packs:** Various bright colored Kona Cotton Solids by Robert Kaufman

- **Fabric A:** Kona Cotton Solids in Charcoal

- **Background fabric:** Kona Cotton Solids in White

This version showcases solids as all of the fabrics in the quilt (charm packs, fabric A, and background fabric) and is perfect to use up your scrap solids you have in your sewing room. The alternate colorway of *Morning Flower Patch* was quilted with a swirl flower-like design.

Somerville Circle

Pieced by Cheryl Brickey and quilted by Bear Creek Quilting Company

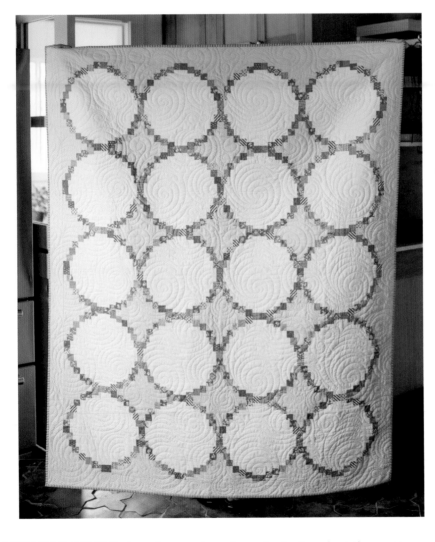

finished quilt

54½″ × 66½″

social media

#SomervilleCircleQuilt

SOMERVILLE CIRCLE does have a lot of small piecing, but the pattern makes mini strip sets out of the charm packs which makes the piecing quicker and more accurate.

FABRICS USED

- **Charm Packs:** *Various red Bonnie and Camille for Moda Fabrics scraps*

- **Fabric A:** *Moda Bella Solids in White*

- **Background fabric:** *Moda Bella Solids in Sister's Pink*

Fabric Requirements

Width of fabrics (WOF) is assumed to be at least 40″.

CHARM SQUARES 5″ × 5″: 65

FABRIC A (WHITE): 2⅜ yards

BACKGROUND (BG) FABRIC (PINK): 1⅞ yards

BINDING: ¾ yard

BACKING FABRIC: 3½ yards

BATTING: 63″ × 75″

Cutting Instructions

CHARM SQUARES

Cut each charm square into 3 rectangles 1½″ × 5″ for a total of 195 rectangles.

FABRIC A (WHITE)

- Cut 5 strips 8½″ × WOF.

  a. Sub-cut the strips into 20 squares 8½″ × 8½″ (each strip can yield 4 squares).

- Cut 7 strips 2″ × WOF.

  a. Sub-cut the strips into 54 rectangles 2″ × 5″ (each strip can yield 8 rectangles).

- Cut 7 strips 1½″ × WOF.

  a. Sub-cut the strips into 54 rectangles 1½″ × 5″ (each strip can yield 8 rectangles).

- Cut 7 strips 1″ × WOF.

  a. Sub-cut the strips into 54 rectangles 1″ × 5″ (each strip can yield 8 rectangles).

BACKGROUND (BG) FABRIC (PINK)

- Cut 2 strips 4½″ × WOF.

  a. Sub-cut the strips into 12 squares 4½″ × 4½″ (each strip can yield 8 squares).

- Cut 9 strips 3″ × WOF.

  a. Sub-cut 1 strip into 8 rectangles 3″ × 4½″.

  b. Sub-cut 1 strip into 6 additional rectangles 3″ × 4½″ and 4 squares 3″ × 3″.

  c. Reserve the remaining 7 strips for the border.

- Cut 3 strips 2½″ × WOF.

  a. Sub-cut the strips into 21 rectangles 2½″ × 5″ (each strip can yield 8 rectangles).

- Cut 2 strips 2″ × WOF.

  a. Sub-cut the strips into 12 rectangles 2″ × 5″ (each strip can yield 8 rectangles).

- Cut 5 strips 1½″ × WOF.

  a. Sub-cut the strips into 33 rectangles 1½″ × 5″ (each strip can yield 8 rectangles).

- Cut 2 strips 1″ × WOF.

  a. Sub-cut the strips into 12 rectangles 1″ × 5″ (each strip can yield 8 rectangles).

BINDING FABRIC

Cut 8 strips 2½″ × WOF.

Piecing Instructions

For all strip sets and blocks, press the seams open or towards the darker fabrics unless otherwise stated.

A scant ¼″ (a thread width smaller than ¼″) seam is to be used throughout the construction of the quilt top unless otherwise instructed.

Strip Set A & Segment A

1. Sew together the following rectangles to make a strip set A 4½″ tall × 5″ wide.

2 charm rectangles 1½″ × 5″

1 bg rectangle 2½″ × 5″

2. Repeat to make a total of 21 strip set A.

3. Cut the strip set A into 62 segment A 1½″ × 4½″ (each strip set can yield 3 segments).

Strip Set B & Segment B

1. Sew together the following rectangles to make a strip set B 4½″ tall × 5″ wide.

2 charm rectangles 1½″ × 5″

2 fabric A rectangles 1″ × 5″

1 bg rectangle 1½″ × 5″

2. Repeat to make a total of 21 strip set B.

3. Cut the strip set B into 62 segment B 1½″ × 4½″ (each strip set can yield 3 segments).

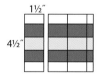

Strip Set C & Segment C

1. Sew together the following rectangles to make a strip set C 4½″ tall × 5″ wide.

2 charm rectangles 1½″ × 5″

2 fabric A rectangles 1½″ × 5″

2. Repeat to make a total of 21 strip set C.

3. Cut the strip set C into 62 segment C 1½″ × 4½″ (each strip set can yield 3 segments).

Strip Set D & Segment D

1. Sew together the following rectangles to make a strip set D 4½″ tall × 5″ wide.

- 1 charm rectangle 1½″ × 5″
- 2 fabric A rectangles 2″ × 5″

2. Repeat to make a total of 21 strip set D.

3. Cut the strip set D into 62 segment D 1½″ × 4½″ (each strip set can yield 3 segments).

Strip Set E & Segment E

1. Sew together the following rectangles to make a strip set E 3″ tall × 5″ wide.

- 1 charm rectangle 1½″ × 5″
- 1 bg rectangle 2″ × 5″

2. Repeat to make a total of 12 strip set E.

3. Cut the strip set E into 36 segment E 1½″ × 3″ (each strip set can yield 3 segments).

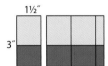

Strip Set F & Segment F

1. Sew together the following rectangles to make a strip set F 3″ tall × 5″ wide.

- 1 charm rectangle 1½″ × 5″
- 1 fabric A rectangle 1″ × 5″
- 1 bg rectangle 1½″ × 5″

2. Repeat to make a total of 12 strip set F.

3. Cut the strip set F into 36 segment F 1½″ × 3″ (each strip set can yield 3 segments).

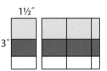

Strip Set G & Segment G

1. Sew together the following rectangles to make a strip set G 3″ tall × 5″ wide.

- 1 charm rectangle 1½″ × 5″
- 1 fabric A rectangle 1½″ × 5″
- 1 bg rectangle 1″ × 5″

2. Repeat to make a total of 12 strip set G.

3. Cut the strip set G into 36 segment G 1½″ × 3″ (each strip set can yield 3 segments).

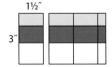

Strip Set H & Segment H

1. Sew together the following rectangles, pressing the seam open, to make a strip set H 3″ tall × 5″ wide.

- 1 charm rectangle 1½″ × 5″
- 1 fabric A rectangle 2″ × 5″

2. Repeat to make a total of 12 strip set H.

3. Cut the strip set H into 36 segment H 1½″ × 3″ (each strip set can yield 3 segments).

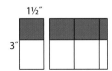

Full Blocks

1. Sew together the following segments to make a full block 4½″ × 8½″.

> 2 segment A 1½″ × 4½″
>
> 2 segment B 1½″ × 4½″
>
> 2 segment C 1½″ × 4½″
>
> 2 segment D 1½″ × 4½″

2. Repeat to make a total of 31 full blocks.

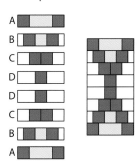

Half Blocks

1. Sew together the following segments to make a half block 3″ × 8½″.

> 2 segment E 1½″ × 3″
>
> 2 segment F 1½″ × 3″
>
> 2 segment G 1½″ × 3″
>
> 2 segment H 1½″ × 3″

2. Repeat to make a total of 18 half blocks.

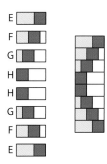

Quilt Top Assembly

Row X

1. Sew together the following blocks and pieces, pressing the seams open or towards the bg fabric, to make a block row X 3″ × 49½″.

> 4 half blocks 3″ × 8½″
>
> 3 bg rectangles 3″ × 4½″
>
> 2 bg squares 3″ × 3″

2. Repeat to make a total of 2 row X.

Row Y

1. Sew together the following blocks and pieces, pressing the seams open or towards the bg fabric, to make a block row Y 8½″ × 49½″.

> 3 full blocks 4½″ × 8½″
>
> 2 half blocks 3″ × 8½″
>
> 4 fabric A squares 8½″ × 8½″

2. Repeat to make a total of 5 row Y.

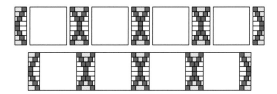

Row Z

1. Sew together the following blocks and pieces, pressing the seams open or towards the bg fabric, to make a block row Z 4½″ × 49½″.

   4 full blocks 4½″ × 8½″

   3 bg squares 4½″ × 4½″

   2 bg rectangles 3″ × 4½″

2. Repeat to make a total of 4 row Z.

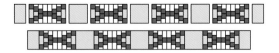

Quilt Top Assembly

1. Sew together the following rows as shown in the quilt top assembly diagram, pressing the seams open, to make the quilt top.

   2 row X 3″ × 49½″

   5 row Y 8½″ × 49½″

   4 row Z 4½″ × 49½″

The quilt top, before the borders are added, should measure approx. 49½″ × 61½″.

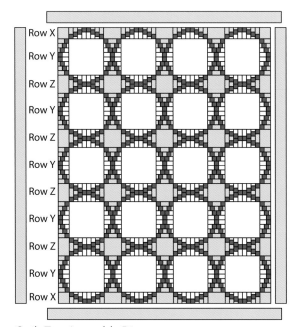

Quilt Top Assembly Diagram

Border

Refer to the Quilt Top Assembly Diagram.

1. Sew together 2 bg strips 3″ × WOF and trim to the average height of the quilt, approx. 61½″. Repeat to make a second border.

2. Sew the borders onto the sides of the quilt top, pressing the seams open or towards the borders.

3. Cut 1 bg strip 3″ × WOF in half and sew each half to a full bg strip 3″ × WOF. Trim to the average width of the quilt, approx. 54½″.

4. Sew the borders onto the top and bottom of the quilt top, pressing the seams open or towards the borders.

The finished quilt top should measure approx. 54½″ × 66½″.

Finishing

Refer to Finishing the Quilt (page 124) for instructions on how to finish the quilt.

1. Make the quilt backing:

Remove selvages, cut into 2 pieces (about 63″ × WOF) and sew backing pieces together along the trimmed selvage edges using a ½″ seam, pressing the seam open. Trim to approx. 63″ × 75″.

2. Layer the quilt top, batting, and backing. Baste and quilt as desired.

The main colorway of the *Somerville Circle* quilt was quilted with a swirl design.

3. Trim off selvages from the binding strips 2½″ × WOF and sew together end-to-end to make the binding. Bind and enjoy your quilt!

alternate colorway

Pieced and quilted
by Yvonne Fuchs

FABRICS USED

- **Charm Packs:** *True Colors by Tula Pink for FreeSpirit Fabrics*
- **Fabric A:** *Fairy Flakes in Paper from the Tula Pink Linework collection for FreeSpirit Fabrics*
- **Background fabric:** *FreeSpirit Tula Pink Solids in Sweet*

Yvonne arranged the Tula Pink prints in rainbow order for the blocks. This took more planning, but creates a stunning affect! The alternate colorway was quilted using stipple and looping designs.

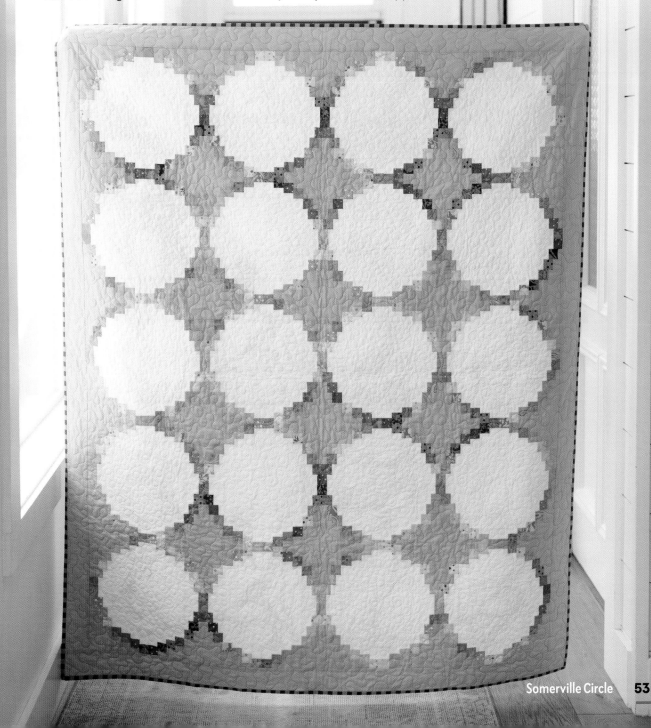

More Fishies

Pieced by Cheryl Brickey and quilted by the Bear Creek Quilting Company

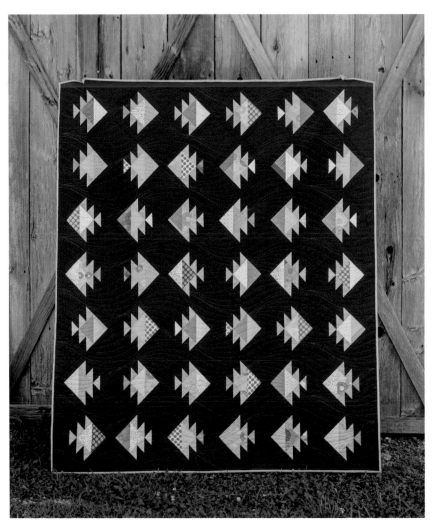

finished block

6″ × 6″

finished quilt

63½″ × 74″

social media

#MoreFishiesQuilt

MY FIRST BOOK about charm packs, Just One Charm Pack, had a quilt with little fish on it called Fishies. It was one of the most popular designs in the book so I had to make *More Fishies!* I also did not have enough of any one print for fabric A, so I used two similarly colored prints together.

FABRICS USED

- **Charm Packs:** *Breeze by Zen Chic for Moda Fabrics plus other blue scraps*
- **Fabric A:** *Mochi—Dottie's Cousin in Lime by Rashida Coleman Hale for Cotton + Steel and Hashdot in Grass by Michael Miller*
- **Background fabric:** *Painters Palette Solids in Midnight by Paintbrush Studios*

Fabric Requirements

Width of fabrics (WOF) is assumed to be at least 40˝.

CHARM SQUARES 5˝ × 5˝: 63

FABRIC A (GREEN): ¾ yard

BACKGROUND (BG) FABRIC (NAVY): 4½ yards

BINDING: ¾ yard

BACKING FABRIC: 4⅝ yards

BATTING: 72˝ × 82˝

Cutting Instructions

CHARM SQUARES

- Trim 21 charm squares to 3˝ × 3˝.

- The remaining 42 charm squares 5˝ × 5˝ will be used without further cutting.

FABRIC A (GREEN)

- Cut 7 strips 3˝ × WOF.

  a. Sub-cut the strips into 84 squares 3˝ × 3˝ (each strip can yield 13 squares).

BACKGROUND (BG) FABRIC (NAVY)

- Cut 2 strips 11¾˝ × WOF.

  a. Sub-cut the strips into 6 squares 11¾˝ × 11¾˝.

  If you like to oversize your setting triangles, then cut your strips to 12¼˝ × WOF and your squares to 12¼˝ × 12¼˝.

- Cut 1 strip 7˝ × WOF.

  Sub-cut the strip into 2 squares 7˝ × 7˝.

  If you like to oversize your setting triangles, then cut your strip to 7½˝ × WOF and your squares to 7½˝ × 7½˝.

- Cut 9 strips 6½˝ × WOF.

  Sub-cut 5 strips into 30 squares 6½˝ × 6½˝ (each strip can yield 6 squares).

  Sub-cut 4 strips into 84 sashing pieces 6½˝ × 1¾˝ (each strip can yield 22 pieces).

- Cut 9 strips 3˝ × WOF.

  a. Sub-cut the strips into 105 squares 3˝ × 3˝ (each strip can yield 13 squares).

- Cut 19 strips 1¾˝ × WOF.

BINDING FABRIC

Cut 8 strips 2½˝ × WOF.

Piecing Instructions

A scant ¼˝ (a thread width smaller than ¼˝) seam is to be used throughout the construction of the quilt top unless otherwise instructed.

Half-Square Triangles Units

1. Place 2 charm squares 5˝ × 5˝ (with different prints) right sides together. Draw a diagonal line using a removable marking device on the back of the lighter square (shown as the solid line).

2. Sew a ¼˝ seam on both sides of the solid line (shown as the dotted lines). Cut on the solid line and press seam open or towards the darker fabric.

3. Trim the charm HST units to 4½˝ × 4½˝. Note: each set of twos charm squares will yield two HST units.

4. Repeat steps 1–3 to make a total of 42 charm/charm HST units 4½˝ × 4½˝.

5. Repeat steps 1–3 using charm squares 3˝ × 3˝ and bg squares 3˝ × 3˝ to make a total of 42 charm/bg HST units 2½˝ × 2½˝.

6. Repeat steps 1–3 using fabric A squares 3˝ × 3˝ and bg squares 3˝ × 3˝ to make a total of 168 fabric A/bg HST units 2½˝ × 2½˝.

Fish Blocks

1. Sew together the following units, pressing the seams open, to make a fish block 6½˝ × 6½˝.

    1 charm/charm HST unit 4½˝ × 4½˝

    1 charm/bg HST unit 2½˝ × 2½˝

    4 A/bg HST units 2½˝ × 2½˝

2. Repeat to make a total of 42 fish blocks.

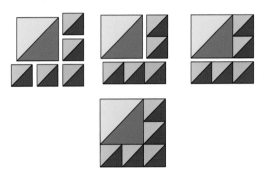

Quilt Top Assembly

During the quilt top assembly, it is recommended to press all seams open or towards the sashing pieces and strips.

Setting And Corner Triangles

1. Cut 6 bg squares 11¾˝ × 11¾˝ (or 12¼˝ × 12¼˝ if you oversized them) on the diagonal twice to make 24 setting triangles (22 will be used in the quilt top).

2. Cut 2 bg squares 7˝ × 7˝ (or 7½˝ × 7½˝ if you oversized them) on the diagonal once to make 4 corner triangles.

Row A

1. Sew together the following pieces and blocks to make a block row 6½″ × 9″.

   1 fish block 6½″ × 6½″

   2 sashing pieces 1¾″ × 6½″

2. From 1 bg strip 1¾″ × WOF, cut 2 sashing rows 1¾″ × 9″ (save the remainder of this strip for a future step).

3. Sew a sashing row 1¾″ × 9″ on the top of the block row, then sew setting triangles on each end to make a row A.

4. Repeat to make a total of 2 row A.

Row B

1. Sew together the following pieces and blocks to make a block row 6½″ × 23½″.

   2 fish blocks 6½″ × 6½″

   1 bg square 6½″ × 6½″

   4 sashing pieces 1¾″ × 6½″

2. Trim 2 bg strips 1¾″ × WOF each to 1¾″ × 23½″ to make 2 sashing rows 1¾″ × 23½″.

3. Sew a sashing row and a block row together, then sew setting triangles on each end, pressing all seams open to make a row B.

4. Repeat to make a total of 2 row B.

Row C

1. Sew together the following pieces and blocks to make a block row 6½″ × 38″.

   3 fish blocks 6½″ × 6½″

   2 bg squares 6½″ × 6½″

   6 sashing pieces 1¾″ × 6½″

2. Trim 2 bg strips 1¾″ × WOF each to 1¾″ × 38″ to make 2 sashing rows 1¾″ × 38″.

3. Sew a sashing row and a block row together, then sew setting triangles on each end, pressing all seams open to make a row C.

4. Repeat to make a total of 2 row C.

Row D

1. Sew together the following pieces and blocks to make a block row 6½″ × 52½″.

   4 fish blocks 6½″ × 6½″

   3 bg squares 6½″ × 6½″

   8 sashing pieces 1¾″ × 6½″

2. Cut 1 bg strip 1¾″ × WOF in half and sew each half to a full bg strip 1¾″ × WOF. Trim each strip to 52½″ to make 2 sashing rows 1¾″ × 52½″.

3. Sew a sashing row and a block row together, then sew setting triangles on each end, pressing all seams open to make a row D.

4. Repeat to make a total of 2 row D.

Row E

1. Sew together the following pieces and blocks to make a block row 6½″ × 67″.

    5 fish blocks 6½″ × 6½″

    4 bg squares 6½″ × 6½″

    10 sashing pieces 1¾″ × 6½″

2. Sew together 2 bg strips 1¾″ × WOF and trim to 67″ to make a sashing row 1¾″ × 67″. Repeat to make a second sashing row.

3. Sew a sashing row and a block row together, then sew setting triangles on each end, pressing all seams open to make a row E.

4. Repeat to make a total of 2 row E.

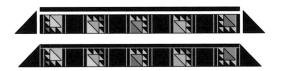

Row F

1. Sew together the following pieces and blocks to make a block row 6½″ × 81½″.

    6 fish blocks 6½″ × 6½″

    5 bg squares 6½″ × 6½″

    12 sashing pieces 1¾″ × 6½″

2. Sew together 2 bg strips 1¾″ × WOF (and some of the leftover strip from row A if needed), then trim to 81½″ to make a sashing row 1¾″ × 81½″. Repeat to make a second sashing row.

3. Sew a sashing row and a block row together, then sew a setting triangle on the right end, pressing all seams open to make a row F.

4. Repeat to make a total of 2 row F.

Row G

Sew together 3 bg strips 1¾″ × WOF and trim to 88¾″ to make a row G 1¾″ × 88¾″.

Note: I suggest cutting this strip a little longer (around 92″ long) and then trimming after the quilt top is assembled.

Quilt Top Assembly

1. Arrange and sew together the rows as shown in the first quilt top assembly diagram to make the quilt top. Some of the rows will be rotated 180 degrees.

2. Referring to the second quilt top assembly diagram, sew the 4 corner triangles onto the corners of the quilt top.

3. Trim the edges of the quilt top even (if needed) making sure that there is at least ¼″ from the seams to the edge of the quilt top.

The quilt top should measure approx. 63½″ × 74″.

Finishing

Refer to Finishing the Quilt (page 124) for instructions on how to finish the quilt.

1. Make the quilt backing:

Remove selvages, cut into 2 pieces (about 82˝ × WOF) and sew backing pieces together along the trimmed selvage edges using a ½˝ seam, pressing the seam open. Trim to approx. 72˝ × 82˝. *Note that the seam in the backing will be vertical.*

2. Layer the quilt top, batting, and backing. Baste and quilt as desired.

The main colorway of the *More Fishies* quilt was quilted with a gentle underwater current design.

3. Trim off selvages from the binding strips 2½˝ × WOF and sew together end-to-end to make the binding. Bind and enjoy your quilt!

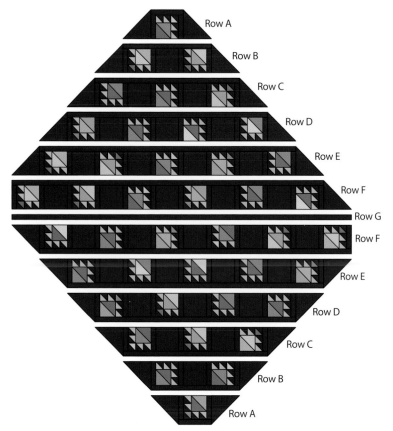

First Quilt Top Assembly Diagram

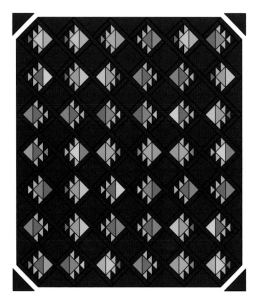

Second Quilt Top Assembly Diagram

alternate colorway

FABRICS USED

- **Charm Packs:** *Various dark blue scraps*
- **Fabric A:** *Sunkissed by Maureen Cracknell for Art Gallery Fabrics*
- **Background fabric:** *Bella Solids in Bluebell by Moda Fabrics*

The alternate colorway of *More Fishies* was quilted with a wave design.

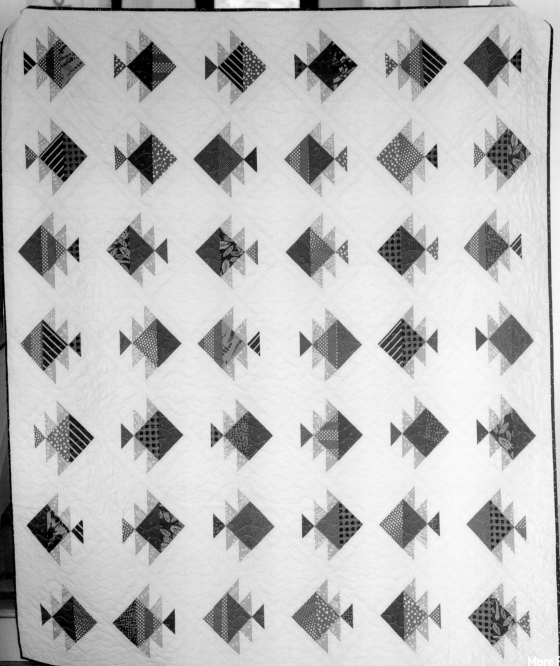

Growing Vines

Pieced by Cheryl Brickey and quilted by Bear Creek Quilting Company

finished block
9″ × 8″

finished quilt
60½″ × 72½″

social media
#GrowingVinesQuilt

GROWING VINES contains instructions for exact placement of the fabric A half-square triangle (HST) units as in the quilt picture, but feel free to change up the number and/or the location of the fabric A HST units. The main colorway has a fun difference compared to many of the other quilts in the book, the solids are the charm squares and the print is the fabric A. The gingham print adds a pop to the quilt.

Fabric Requirements

Width of fabrics (WOF) is assumed to be at least 40˝.

CHARM SQUARES 5˝ × 5˝: 75

FABRIC A (PLAID): ¼ yard

BACKGROUND (BG) FABRIC (CREAM): 3½ yards

BINDING: ⅝ yard

BACKING FABRIC: 3⅞ yards

BATTING: 69˝ × 80˝

Cutting Instructions

CHARM SQUARES

- Cut 30 charm squares each into 3 rectangles 1½˝ × 4½˝ for a total of 90 rectangles.

- The remaining 45 charm squares 5˝ × 5˝ will be used without further cutting.

FABRIC A (PLAID)

Note: The plaid print for fabric A is shown as a solid dark brown in the instructions.

- Cut 1 strips 5˝ × WOF.
  a. Sub-cut the strip into 6 squares 5˝ × 5˝.

BACKGROUND (BG) FABRIC (CREAM)

- Cut 7 strips 5˝ × WOF.
  a. Sub-cut the strips into 51 squares 5˝ × 5˝ (each strip can yield 8 squares).

- Cut 10 strips 4½˝ × WOF.
  a. Sub-cut the strips into 78 squares 4½˝ × 4½˝ (each strip can yield 8 squares).

- Cut 12 strips 3˝ × WOF.

BINDING FABRIC

Cut 7 strips 2½˝ × WOF.

Piecing Instructions

A scant ¼˝ (a thread width smaller than ¼˝) seam is to be used throughout the construction of the quilt top unless otherwise instructed.

Half-Square Triangles Units

1. Place a charm square 5˝ × 5˝ and a bg square 5˝ × 5˝ right sides together. Draw a diagonal line using a removable marking device on the back of the lighter square (shown as the solid line).

2. Sew a ¼˝ seam on both sides of the solid line (shown as the dotted lines). Cut on the solid line and press seam open or towards the darker fabric.

3. Trim the charm HST units to 4½˝ × 4½˝. Note: each set of one charm square and one bg square will yield two HST units.

4. Repeat steps 1–3 to make a total of 90 charm HST units 4½˝ × 4½˝.

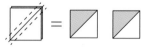

5. Repeat steps 1–3 using fabric A squares and bg squares 5˝ × 5˝ to make a total of 12 fabric A HST units 4½˝ × 4½˝.

Block A

1. Sew together the following pieces and units, pressing the seams open or as indicated by the arrows, to make a block A 9½″ wide by 8½″ tall.

    2 charm HST units 4½″ × 4½″

    2 charm rectangles 1½″ × 4½″

    2 bg squares 4½″ × 4½″

2. Repeat to make a total of 33 block A.

Block B

1. Sew together the following pieces and units, pressing the seams open or as indicated by the arrows, to make a block B 9½″ wide by 8½″ tall.

    2 charm HST units 4½″ × 4½″

    2 charm rectangles 1½″ × 4½″

    1 fabric A HST unit 4½″ × 4½″

    1 bg square 4½″ × 4½″

2. Repeat to make a total of 7 block B.

Block C

1. Sew together the following pieces and units, pressing the seams open or as indicated by the arrows, to make a block C 9½″ wide by 8½″ tall.

    2 charm HST units 4½″ × 4½″

    2 charm rectangles 1½″ × 4½″

    1 fabric A HST unit 4½″ × 4½″

    1 bg square 4½″ × 4½″.

2. Repeat to make a total of 5 block C.

Quilt Top Assembly

Block Columns

Sew together the following blocks listed in the table and shown in the Column Assembly Diagram, pressing the seams open, to make the column rows 9½″ × 72½″.

Block Column 1	6 Block A 1 Block B 2 Block C
Block Column 2	8 Block A 1 Block B
Block Column 3	6 Block A 3 Block B
Block Column 4	7 Block A 1 Block B 1 Block C
Block Column 5	6 Block A 1 Block B 2 Block C

Diagram on next page ⟶

Sashing Columns

1. Sew together 2 bg strips 3˝ × WOF and trim to the average height of the block columns, approx. 72½˝, to make a sashing column 3˝ × 72½˝.

2. Repeat to make a total of 6 sashing columns.

Quilt Top Assembly

Sew together the 5 block columns and 6 sashing columns as shown in the quilt top assembly diagram, pressing seams open or towards the sashing columns, to make the quilt top.

The quilt top should measure approx. 60½˝ × 72½˝.

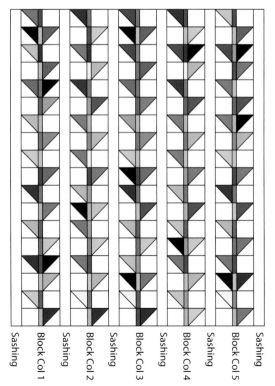

Quilt Top Assembly Diagram

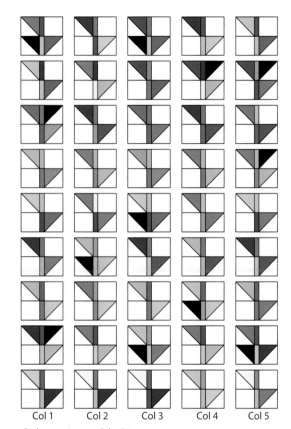

Column Assembly Diagram

Finishing

Refer to Finishing the Quilt (page 124) for instructions on how to finish the quilt.

1. Make the quilt backing:

Remove selvages, cut into 2 pieces (about 69˝ × WOF) and sew backing pieces together along the trimmed selvage edges using a ½˝ seam, pressing the seam open. Trim to approx. 69˝ × 80˝.

2. Layer the quilt top, batting, and backing. Baste and quilt as desired. The main colorway of the *Growing Vines* quilt was quilted with a vine design.

3. Trim off selvages from the binding strips 2½˝ × WOF and sew together end-to-end to make the binding. Bind and enjoy your quilt!

alternate colorway

Pieced and quilted
by Cindy Clifton

FABRICS USED

- **Charm Packs:** *Nantucket Summer by Camille Roskelley for Moda Fabrics*
- **Fabric A:** *Bella Solids in Hunter by Moda Fabrics*
- **Background fabric:** *Bella Solids in White by Moda Fabrics*

The alternate colorway of the *Growing Vines* quilt was quilted with a stipple design.

Star Rays

Pieced by Cheryl Brickey and quilted by Bear Creek Quilting Company

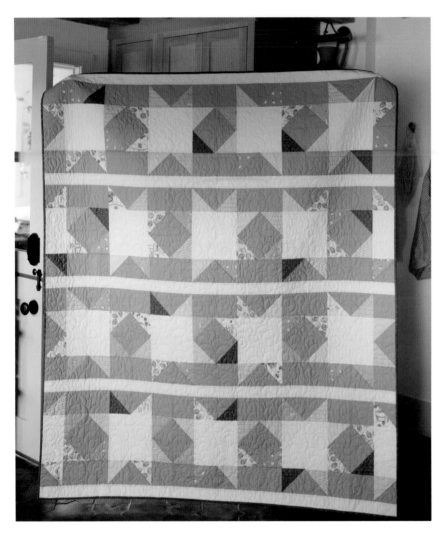

finished block

16˝ × 16˝

finished quilt

64½˝ × 74½˝

social media

#StarRaysQuilt

STAR QUILTS are one of my favorites and I really like how these blocks are offset and placed in rows. For this design, the charm squares are right next to both the fabric A and the background so be sure to pick supporting fabrics that have good contrast with the charm squares.

FABRICS USED

- **Charm Packs:** *Sunburst by AGF Studio for Art Gallery Fabrics*
- **Fabric A:** *Pure Solids in Ocean Waves by Art Gallery Fabrics*
- **Background fabric:** *Pure Solids in Snow by Art Gallery Fabrics*

Fabric Requirements

Width of fabrics (WOF) is assumed to be at least 40˝.

CHARM SQUARES 5˝ × 5˝: 64

FABRIC A (BLUE): 2⅜ yards

BACKGROUND (BG) FABRIC (WHITE): 2 yards

BINDING: ¾ yard

BACKING FABRIC: 4⅔ yards

BATTING: 73˝ × 83˝

Cutting Instructions

CHARM SQUARES

The charm squares 5˝ × 5˝ will be used without further cutting.

FABRIC A (BLUE)

- Cut 8 strips 5˝ × WOF.

  a. Sub-cut the strips into 64 squares 5˝ × 5˝ (each strip can yield 8 squares).

- Cut 8 strips 4½˝ × WOF.

  a. Sub-cut the strips into 64 squares 4½˝ × 4½˝ (each strip can yield 8 squares).

BACKGROUND (BG) FABRIC (WHITE)

- Cut 4 strips 8½˝ × WOF.

  a. Sub-cut 3 strips into 12 squares 8½˝ × 8½˝ (each strip can yield 4 squares).

  b. Sub-cut 1 strip into 2 additional squares 8½˝ × 8½˝ and 4 rectangles 8½˝ × 4½˝.

- Cut 10 strips 2½˝ × WOF.

BINDING FABRIC

Cut 8 strips 2½˝ × WOF.

Piecing Instructions

A scant ¼˝ (a thread width smaller than ¼˝) seam is to be used throughout the construction of the quilt top unless otherwise instructed.

Half-Square Triangles Units

1. Place a charm square 5˝ × 5˝ and a fabric A square 5˝ × 5˝ right sides together. Draw a diagonal line using a removable marking device on the back of the lighter square (shown as the solid line).

2. Sew a ¼˝ seam on both sides of the solid line (shown as the dotted lines). Cut on the solid line and press seam open or towards the darker fabric.

3. Trim the HST units to 4½˝ × 4½˝. Note: each set of one charm square and one fabric A square will yield two HST units.

4. Repeat steps 1–3 to make a total of 128 HST units 4½˝ × 4½˝.

Full Blocks

1. Sew together the following units and pieces as listed and shown, pressing seams open to make a full block 16½″ × 16½″.

   8 HST units 4½″ × 4½″

   4 fabric A squares 4½″ × 4½″

   1 bg square 8½″ × 8½″

2. Repeat to make a total of 14 full blocks.

Half Blocks

1. Sew together the following units and pieces as listed and shown, pressing seams open to make a half block 8½″ × 16½″.

   4 HST units 4½″ × 4½″

   2 fabric A squares 4½″ × 4½″

   1 bg rectangle 4½″ × 8½″

2. Repeat to make a total of 4 half blocks.

Quilt Top Assembly

First Block Rows

Sew together 4 full blocks 16½″ × 16½″, pressing the seams open, to make a first block row 16½″ × 64½″. Repeat to make 2 first blocks rows.

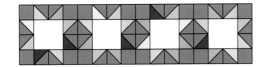

Second Block Rows

Sew together 3 full blocks 16½″ × 16½″ and 2 half blocks 8½″ × 16½″, pressing the seams open, to make a second block row 16½″ × 64½″. Repeat to make 2 second block rows.

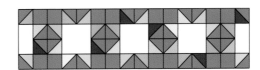

Sashing Rows

1. Sew together 2 bg strips 2½″ × WOF and trim to the average width of the first and second block rows (approx. 64½″) to make a sashing row 2½″ × 64½″.

2. Repeat to make a total of 5 sashing rows.

Quilt Top Assembly

Sew together the following rows as shown in the quilt top assembly diagram, pressing the seams open or towards the sashing rows, to make the quilt top.

2 first block rows 16½″ × 64½″

2 second block rows 16½″ × 64½″

5 sashing rows 2½″ × 64½″

The quilt top should measure approx. 64½″ × 74½″.

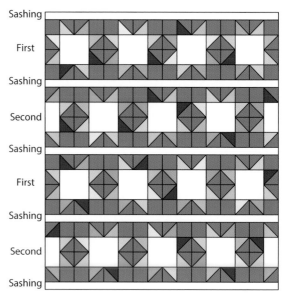

Quilt Top Assembly Diagram

Sashing, First, Sashing, Second, Sashing, First, Sashing, Second, Sashing

Finishing

Refer to Finishing the Quilt (page 124) for instructions on how to finish the quilt.

1. Make the quilt backing:

Remove selvages, cut into 2 pieces (about 83″ × WOF) and sew backing pieces together along the trimmed selvage edges using a ½″ seam, pressing the seam open. Trim to approx. 73″ × 83″. Note: The seam will be vertical in the backing.

2. Layer the quilt top, batting, and backing. Baste and quilt as desired. The main colorway of the Star Ray quilt was quilted with a wave swirl design.

3. Trim off selvages from the binding strips 2½″ × WOF and sew together end-to-end to make the binding. Bind and enjoy your quilt!

alternate colorway

Pieced by Dale Hernandez and quilted by the Carolina Quilt Studio

FABRICS USED

- **Charm Packs:** *One charm pack each of Elixir and Camellia by Melody Miller for Ruby Star Society*
- **Fabric A:** *Add It Up by Alexia Abegg for Ruby Star Society*
- **Background fabric:** *Bella Solids in White by Moda Fabrics*

The alternate colorway of the *Star Ray* quilt was quilted with a combination of an orange peel and swirl design.

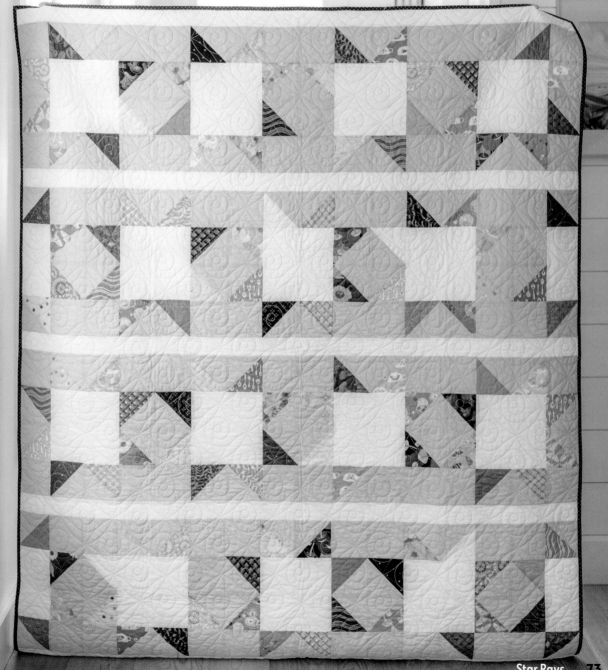

Diagonal Joy

Pieced and quilted by
Cindy Lange

finished block
8″ × 8″

finished quilt
64½″ × 72½″

social media
#DiagonalJoyQuilt

WHEN THE BLOCKS from *Diagonal Joy* are sewn together, the design has a diagonal look to it. Because the charm squares are cut into 2½″ × 2½″ squares, you could also use smaller scraps or part of a jelly roll for this quilt.

FABRICS USED

- **Charm Packs:** *Marmalade by Bonnie and Camille for Moda Fabrics*
- **Fabric A:** *Bella Solids in White by Moda Fabrics*
- **Background fabric:** *Bella Solids in Stone by Moda Fabrics*

Fabric Requirements

Width of fabrics (WOF) is assumed to be at least 40˝.

CHARM SQUARES 5˝ × 5˝: 72

FABRIC A (WHITE): 1¼ yards

BACKGROUND (BG) FABRIC (GRAY): 3½ yards

BINDING: ¾ yard

BACKING FABRIC: 41/8 yards

BATTING: 73˝ × 80˝

Cutting Instructions

CHARM SQUARES

Cut each charm square 5˝ × 5˝ in half once horizontally and vertically to make matching squares 2½˝ × 2½˝, for a total of 288 squares 2½˝ × 2½˝.

You could instead use jelly roll strips (2½ × WOF) or scraps cut into 288 squares 2½˝ × 2½˝ instead of charm squares.

FABRIC A (WHITE)

- Cut 5 strips 5˝ × WOF.

  a. Sub-cut the strips into 36 squares 5˝ × 5˝ (each strip can yield 8 squares).

- Cut 5 strips 2½˝ × WOF.

  a. Sub-cut the strips into 72 squares 2½˝ × 2½˝ (each strip can yield 16 squares).

BACKGROUND (BG) FABRIC (GRAY)

- Cut 5 strips 5˝ × WOF.

  a. Sub-cut the strips into 36 squares 5˝ × 5˝ (each strip can yield 8 squares).

- Cut 36 strips 2½˝ × WOF.

  a. Sub-cut 18 strips into 144 rectangles 2½˝ × 4½˝ (each strip can yield 8 rectangles).

  b. Sub-cut 18 strips into 288 squares 2½˝ × 2½˝ (each strip can yield 16 squares).

BINDING FABRIC

Cut 8 strips 2½˝ × WOF.

Piecing Instructions

A scant ¼˝ (a thread width smaller than ¼˝) seam is to be used throughout the construction of the quilt top unless otherwise instructed.

Triangle Units

1. Place a fabric A square 5˝ × 5˝ and a bg square 5˝ × 5˝ right sides together. Draw a diagonal line using a removable marking device on the back of the lighter square (shown as the solid line).

2. Sew a ¼˝ seam on both sides of the solid line (shown as the dotted lines). Cut on the solid line and press seam open or towards the darker fabric.

3. Trim the half-square triangles (HST) to 4½˝ × 4½˝. Note: each set of one fabric A square and one bg square will yield two HSTs.

4. Place a fabric A square 2½″ × 2½″ in the bg triangle of the half-square triangle right sides together. Draw a diagonal line on the back of the fabric A square using a removable marking device.

5. Sew on the marked line (shown as the dotted line), trim a ¼″ from the stitched line and press the seam open or towards the fabric A to make a triangle unit 4½″ × 4½″.

6. Repeat steps 1–5 to make a total of 72 triangle units.

Corner Units

1. Sew together the following pieces, pressing all seams open or towards the bg fabric, to make a corner unit 4½″ × 4½″.

 1 charm square 2½″ × 2½″

 1 bg rectangle 2½″ × 4½″

 1 bg square 2½″ × 2½″

2. Repeat to make a total of 72 corner units.

Block A

1. Sew together the following units, pressing the seams open or towards the corner units, to make a block A 8½″ × 8½″.

 2 triangle units 4½″ × 4½″

 2 corner units 4½″ × 4½″

2. Repeat to make a total of 36 block A.

First Units

1. Sew together the following pieces, pressing the seams open or towards the bg fabric, to make a first unit 2½″ × 8½″.

 1 charm square 2½″ × 2½″

 1 bg rectangle 2½″ × 4½″

 1 bg square 2½″ × 2½″

2. Repeat to make a total of 72 first units.

Second Units

1. Sew together the following pieces, pressing the seams open or towards the bg fabric, to make a first unit 2½″ × 8½″.

 2 charm squares 2½″ × 2½″

 2 bg squares 2½″ × 2½″

2. Repeat to make a total of 72 second units.

Block B

1. Sew together the following units, pressing the seams open, to make a block B 8½″ × 8½″.

    2 first units 2½″ × 8½″

    2 second units 2½″ × 8½″

2. Repeat to make a total of 36 block B.

Quilt Top Assembly

1. Sew together the following blocks, pressing the seams open or towards the block B, to make a block row 8½″ × 64½″.

    4 block A 8½″ × 8½″

    4 block B 8½″ × 8½″

2. Repeat to make a total of 9 block rows.

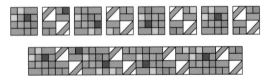

3. Arrange and sew together the 9 block rows as shown in the quilt top assembly diagram, pressing the seams open, to make the quilt top. *Some of the block rows will be rotated 180 degrees.*

The quilt top should measure approx. 64½″ × 72½″.

Finishing

Refer to Finishing the Quilt (page 124) for instructions on how to finish the quilt.

1. Make the quilt backing:

Remove selvages, cut into 2 pieces (about 73″ × WOF) and sew backing pieces together along the trimmed selvage edges using a ½″ seam, pressing the seam open. Trim to approx. 73″ × 80″.

2. Layer the quilt top, batting, and backing. Baste and quilt as desired. The main colorway of the *Diagonal Joy* quilt was quilted with a cross-hatch straight line design.

3. Trim off selvages from the binding strips 2½″ × WOF and sew together end-to-end to make the binding. Bind and enjoy your quilt!

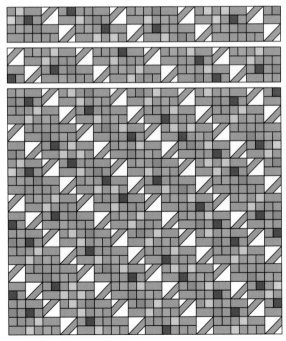

Quilt Top Assembly Diagram

FABRICS USED

- **Charm Packs:** *Oh Deer by MoMo for Moda Fabrics*
- **Fabric A:** *Bella Solids in Prussian Blue by Moda Fabrics*
- **Background fabric:** *Bella Solids in White by Moda Fabrics*

The alternate colorway of the *Diagonal Joy* quilt was quilted with a double looping design.

Process Flow

Pieced by Cheryl Brickey and quilted by the Bear Creek Quilting Company

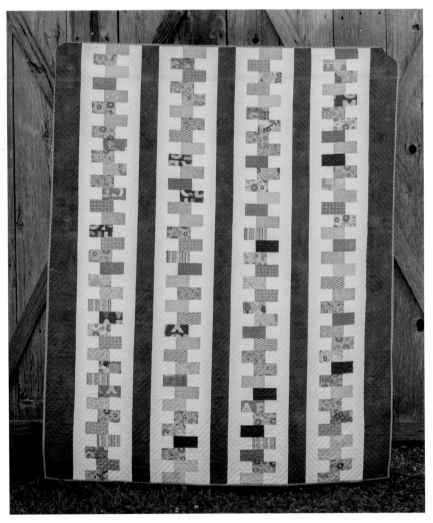

finished block

6″ × 12″

finished quilt

59½″ × 72½″

social media

#ProcessFlowQuilt

PROCESS FLOW is a great and quick quilt with very few seams to match. It is perfect for a beginner or as a quicker finished for an advanced quilter.

FABRICS USED

- **Charm Packs:** *PB&J by Basic Gray for Moda Fabrics*
- **Fabric A:** *Bella Solids in White by Moda Fabrics*
- **Background fabric:** *Grunge in Picnic by Moda Fabrics*

Fabric Requirements

Width of fabrics (WOF) is assumed to be at least 40˝.

CHARM SQUARES 5˝ × 5˝: 72

FABRIC A (WHITE): 2 yards

BACKGROUND (BG) FABRIC (NAVY): 1½ yards

BINDING: ⅝ yard

BACKING FABRIC: 3⅞ yards

BATTING: 68˝ × 80˝

Cutting Instructions

CHARM SQUARES

Cut each charm square into 2 rectangles 2½˝ × 4½˝ for a total of 144 rectangles.

Note: You could also use 18 jelly roll strips (2½˝ × WOF) or scraps cut into 144 rectangles 2½˝ × 4½˝.

FABRIC A (WHITE)

- Cut 25 strips 2½˝ × WOF.
  a. Sub-cut 9 strips into 144 squares 2½˝ × 2½ (each strip can yield 16 squares).
  b. Reserve the remaining 16 strips.

BACKGROUND (BG) FABRIC (NAVY)

- Cut 4 strips 5½˝ × WOF.
- Cut 6 stripes 3½˝ × WOF.

BINDING FABRIC

- Cut 7 strips 2½˝ × WOF.

Piecing Instructions

A scant ¼˝ (a thread width smaller than ¼˝) seam is to be used throughout the construction of the quilt top unless otherwise instructed.

Block Assembly

None of the seams within the block or quilt top nest or line up, so the seams can be pressed open or towards the darker fabric.

1. Sew together 1 charm rectangle 2½˝ × 4½˝ and 1 fabric A square 2½˝ × 2½˝ to make a unit 2½˝ × 6½˝.

2. Repeat to make a total of 144 units.

3. Sew together 6 units 2½˝ × 4½˝ as shown to make a block 6½˝ × 12½˝.

Be sure that a charm rectangle is in the upper right hand corner of each block.

4. Repeat to make a total of 24 blocks.

Block Columns

1. Sew together 6 blocks to make a block column 6½ × 72½.

2. Repeat to make a total of 4 block columns.

Sashing Assembly

1. Sew together 2 fabric A strips 2½″ × WOF and trim to the height of the block columns (approx. 72½″) to make a sashing column 2½″ × 72½″.

2. Repeat to make a total of 8 sashing columns.

Inner bg Columns

1. Sew together 2 bg strips 3½″ × WOF and trim to the height of the block columns (approx. 72½″) to make an inner bg column 3½″ × 72½″.

2. Repeat to make a total of 3 inner bg columns.

Outer bg Columns

1. Sew together 2 bg strips 5½″ × WOF and trim to the height of the block columns (approx. 72½″) to make an outer bg column 5½″ × 72½″.

2. Repeat to make a total of 2 outer bg columns.

Quilt Top Assembly

Arrange and sew together the columns listed and as shown in the quilt top assembly diagram, pressing seams open to towards the darker fabrics, to make the finished quilt top 59½″ × 72½″.

  4 block columns 6½″ × 72½″

  8 sashing columns 2½″ × 72½″

  3 inner bg columns 3½″ × 72½″

  2 outer bg columns 5½″ × 72½″

Finishing

Refer to Finishing the Quilt (page 124) for instructions on how to finish the quilt.

1. Make the quilt backing:

Remove selvages, cut into 2 pieces (about 68″ × WOF) and sew backing pieces together along the trimmed selvage edges using a ½″ seam, pressing the seam open. Trim to approx. 68″ × 80″.

2. Layer the quilt top, batting, and backing. Baste and quilt as desired. The main colorway of *Process Flow* was quilted with a maze-like design.

3. Trim off selvages from the binding strips 2½″ × WOF and sew together end-to-end to make the binding. Bind and enjoy your quilt!

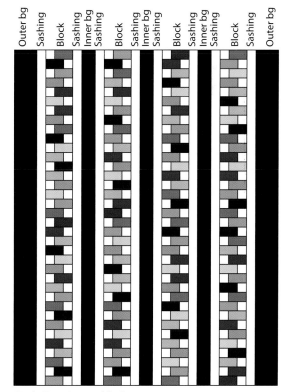

Quilt Top Assembly Diagram

alternate colorway

Pieced and quilted by Darleen Sanford

FABRICS USED

- **Charm Packs:** *Daydreamer by Tula Pink for FreeSpirit Fabrics*
- **Fabric A:** *FreeSpirit Solids in White by FreeSpirit Fabrics*
- **Background fabric:** *Tula Pink Solids in Dazzle for FreeSpirit Fabrics*

The alternate colorway of *Process Flow* was quilted with a back and forth and wavy designs.

Taylors Square

Pieced and quilted by
Cheryl Brickey

finished block
12″ × 12″

finished quilt
60½″ × 72½″

social media
#TaylorsSquareQuilt

I FELL IN LOVE with the Squeeze collection a few months after it was released but I was not able to find charm squares available, so I bought and cut up a fat quarter bundle of the collection. When cutting up a fat quarter bundle, you can use the remainder of the fat quarters to make a pieced backing or save them for another project.

Fabric Requirements

Width of fabrics (WOF) is assumed to be at least 40˝.

CHARM SQUARES 5˝ × 5˝: 60

FABRIC A (GRAY): 1⅝ yards

BACKGROUND (BG) FABRIC (WHITE): 3¼ yards

BINDING: ⅝ yard

BACKING FABRIC: 3⅞ yards

BATTING: 69˝ × 80˝

Cutting Instructions

CHARM SQUARES

No cutting required, charm squares will be used as 5˝ × 5˝ pieces.

FABRIC A (GRAY)

- Cut 9 strips 5½˝ × WOF.

  a. Sub-cut the strips into 60 squares 5½˝ × 5½˝ (each strip can yield 7 squares).

BACKGROUND (BG) FABRIC (WHITE)

- Cut 9 strips 5½˝ × WOF.

  a. Sub-cut the strips into 60 squares 5½˝ × 5½˝ (each strip can yield 7 squares).

- Cut 8 strips 5˝ × WOF.

  a. Sub-cut the strips into 60 squares 5˝ × 5˝ (each strip can yield 8 squares).

- Cut 4 strips 4½˝ × WOF.

  a. Sub-cut the strips into 30 squares 4½˝ × 4½˝ (each strip can yield 8 squares).

BINDING FABRIC

Cut 7 strips 2½˝ × WOF.

Piecing Instructions

A scant ¼˝ (a thread width smaller than ¼˝) seam is to be used throughout the construction of the quilt top unless otherwise instructed.

Half-Square Triangle (HST) Units

1. Place a charm square 5˝ × 5˝ and a bg square 5˝ × 5˝ right sides together. Draw a diagonal line using a removable marking device on the back of the lighter square (shown as the solid line).

2. Sew a ¼˝ seam on both sides of the solid line (shown as the dotted lines). Cut on the solid line and press the seam open or towards the darker fabric.

3. Trim the HST units to 4½˝ × 4½˝. Note: each set of one charm square and one bg square will yield two HST units.

4. Repeat steps 1–3 to make a total of 120 HST units 4½˝ × 4½˝.

Hourglass Units

1. Place a fabric A square 5½˝ × 5½˝ and a bg square 5½˝ × 5½˝ right sides together.

Draw a diagonal line using a removable marking device on the back of the lighter square (shown as the solid line).

2. Sew a ¼˝ seam on both sides of the solid line (shown as the dotted lines). Cut on the solid line and press seam towards the darker fabric. Do not trim these half-square triangles.

FABRICS USED

- **Charm Packs:** *Squeeze collection by Dana Willard for Figo Fabrics*
- **Fabric A:** *Canvas in Charcoal by Deborah Edwards for Northcott Fabrics*
- **Background fabric:** *Colorworks Solids in Superwhite by Northcott Fabrics*

3. Repeat steps 1–2 to make a total of 120 HST measuring about 5˝ × 5˝.

4. Place 2 HST right sides together such that the seams nest together and HST are oriented as shown in the illustration.

5. Draw a diagonal line using a removable marking device on the back of the one of the HST (shown as the solid line) perpendicular to the seam of that HST.

6. Sew a ¼˝ seam on each side of the solid line (shown as the dotted lines). Cut on the solid line and press seams open.

7. Trim the hourglass units to 4½˝ × 4½˝.

8. Repeat steps 4–7 to make a total of 120 hourglass units 4½˝ × 4½˝.

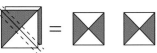

Block Assembly

1. Sew together the following units and pieces as listed and shown, pressing the seams open, to make a block 12½˝ × 12½˝.

4 HST units 4½˝ × 4½˝

4 hourglass units 4½˝ × 4½˝

1 bg square 4½˝ × 4½˝

tip **REDUCE BULK**

Because the of the bulky seams and the way the blocks are sewn together, I recommend pressing the seams open to help reduce bulk and make the blocks and quilt top lay flatter.

2. Repeat to make a total of 30 blocks.

Quilt Top Assembly

1. Arrange the blocks in a 5 × 6 arrangement (6 rows of 5 blocks each).

2. Sew the blocks into rows and then sew the rows together, pressing all seams open, to make the quilt top.

The finished quilt top should measure approx. 60½˝ × 72½˝.

Quilt top assembly diagram

Finishing

Refer to Finishing the Quilt (page 124) for instructions on how to finish the quilt.

1. Make the quilt backing: Remove selvages, cut into 2 pieces (about 69˝ × WOF) and sew backing pieces together along the trimmed selvage edges using a ½˝ seam, pressing the seam open. Trim to approx. 69˝ × 80˝.

2. Layer the quilt top, batting, and backing. Baste and quilt as desired. The main colorway of the *Taylors Square* quilt was quilted with a stipple design.

3. Trim off selvages from the binding strips 2 1/2″ × WOF and sew together end-to-end to make the binding. Bind and enjoy your quilt!

alternate colorway

Pieced by Ruth Freyer and quilted by Carol Alperin

FABRICS USED

- **Charm Packs:** *Spooky Darlings by Ruby Star Society for Moda Fabrics*
- **Fabric A:** *Bella Solids in White by Moda Fabrics*
- **Background fabric:** *Grunge in Black Dress by Moda Fabrics*

I love the Halloween version of *Taylors Square* and could see a Christmas or patriotic version too. The alternate colorway of the *Taylors Square* quilt was quilted with a spider web design.

Carnegie Plaid

Pieced and quilted by
Cheryl Brickey

finished block

10″ × 10″

finished quilt

61½″ × 75½″

social media

#CarnegiePlaidQuilt

THIS QUILT gets its name from my college, Carnegie Mellon University, where we did not have official university colors but had an official school plaid.

Fabric Requirements

Width of fabrics (WOF) is assumed to be at least 40˝.

CHARM SQUARES 5˝ × 5˝: 80

FABRIC A (WHITE): 1 yard

BACKGROUND (BG) FABRIC (GRAY): 3 yards

BINDING: ¾ yard

BACKING FABRIC: 4⅔ yards

BATTING: 70˝ × 84˝

Cutting Instructions

CHARM SQUARES

Trim all 80 charm squares to 4½˝ × 4½˝.

FABRIC A (WHITE)

- Cut 5 strips 4½˝ × WOF.

  a. Sub-cut 2 strips into 12 squares 4½˝ × 4½˝.

  b. Sub-cut 3 strips into 45 rectangles 4½˝ × 2½˝ (each strip can yield 16 rectangles).

- Cut 3 strips 2½˝ × WOF.

  a. Sub-cut the strips into 42 squares 2½˝ × 2½˝ (each strip can yield 16 squares).

BACKGROUND (BG) FABRIC (GRAY)

- Cut 16 strips 4½˝ × WOF.

  a. Sub-cut 8 strips into 62 squares 4½˝ × 4½˝ (each strip can yield 8 squares).

  b. Sub-cut 8 strips into 116 rectangles 4½˝ × 2½˝ (each strip can yield 16 rectangles).

- Cut 8 strips 3˝ × WOF for the border.

BINDING FABRIC

Cut 8 strips 2½˝ × WOF.

Piecing Instructions

A scant ¼˝ (a thread width smaller than ¼˝) seam is to be used throughout the construction of the quilt top unless otherwise instructed.

Block Assembly

1. Sew together the following pieces, pressing seams open or as shown by the arrows, to make a block 10½˝ × 10½˝.

   4 charm squares 4½˝ × 4½˝

   1 fabric A square 2½˝ × 2½˝

   4 bg rectangles 2½˝ × 4½˝

2. Repeat to make a total of 20 blocks.

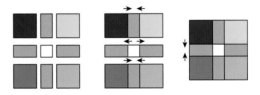

Thin Units

1. Sew together the following pieces, pressing seams open or towards the bg pieces, to make a thin unit 2½˝ × 10½˝.

   1 fabric A square 2½˝ × 2½˝

   2 bg rectangles 2½˝ × 4½˝

2. Repeat to make a total of 18 thin units.

Wide Units

1. Sew together the following pieces, pressing seams open or towards the bg pieces, to make a wide unit 4½˝ × 10½˝.

   1 fabric A rectangle 2½˝ × 4½˝

   2 bg squares 4½˝ × 4½˝

2. Repeat to make a total of 31 wide units.

FABRICS USED

- **Charm Packs:** *Velvet by Amy Sinibald for Art Gallery Fabrics*
- **Fabric A:** *Pure Solids in Snow by Art Gallery Fabrics*
- **Background fabric:** *Decostitch in Shadow by Art Gallery Fabrics*

Quilt Top Assembly

Block Rows

1. Sew together the following blocks and units, pressing the seams open or away from the blocks, to make a block row 10½″ × 56½″.

> 4 blocks 10½″ × 10½″
>
> 2 thin units 2½″ × 10½″
>
> 3 wide units 4½″ × 10½″

2. Repeat to make a total of 5 block rows.

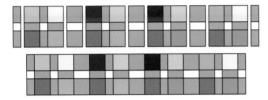

Outer Sashing Rows

1. Sew together the following units and pieces, pressing the seams open or towards the thin units, to make an outer sashing row 2½″ × 56½″.

> 4 thin units 2½″ × 10½″
>
> 2 fabric A squares 2½″ × 2½″
>
> 3 fabric A rectangles 2½″ × 4½″

2. Repeat to make a total of 2 outer sashing rows.

Inner Sashing Rows

1. Sew together the following units and pieces, pressing the seams open or towards the wide units, to make an outer sashing row 4½″ × 56½″.

> 4 wide units 4½″ × 10½″
>
> 3 fabric A squares 4½″ × 4½″
>
> 2 fabric A rectangles 2½″ × 4½″

2. Repeat to make a total of 4 inner sashing rows.

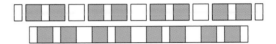

Quilt Top Assembly

Sew together the following rows as shown in the quilt top assembly diagram, pressing the seams open, to make the quilt top.

> 5 block rows 10½″ × 56½″
>
> 2 outer sashing rows 2½″ × 56½″
>
> 4 inner sashing rows 4½″ × 56½″

The quilt top, before the borders are added, should measure approx. 56½″ × 70½″.

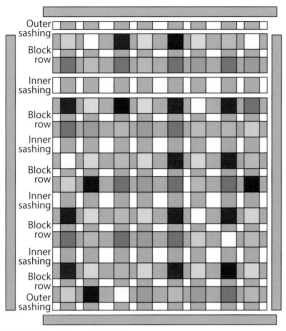

Outer sashing
Block row
Inner sashing
Block row
Inner sashing
Block row
Inner sashing
Block row
Inner sashing
Block row
Outer sashing

Quilt Top Assembly Diagram

Border

1. Sew together 2 bg strips 3″ × WOF and trim to the average height of the quilt, approx. 70½″. Repeat to make a second border.

2. Sew the borders onto the sides of the quilt top, pressing seams open or towards the borders.

3. Sew together 2 bg strips 3″ × WOF and trim to the average width of the quilt, approx. 61½″. Repeat to make a second border.

4. Sew the borders onto the top and bottom of the quilt top, pressing seams open or towards the borders.

The finished quilt top should measure approx. 61½″ × 75½″.

Finishing

Refer to Finishing the Quilt (page 124) for instructions on how to finish the quilt.

1. Make the quilt backing:

Remove selvages, cut into 2 pieces (about 84″ × WOF) and sew backing pieces together along the trimmed selvage edges using a ½″ seam, pressing the seam open. Trim to approx. 70″ × 84″. *Note that the seam will be vertical in the backing.*

2. Layer the quilt top, batting, and backing. Baste and quilt as desired.

The main colorway of the *Carnegie Plaid* quilt was quilted with a bear claw hook design.

3. Trim off selvages from the binding strips 2½″ × WOF and sew together end-to-end to make the binding. Bind and enjoy your quilt!

alternate colorway

Pieced and quilted by Garen Sherwood

FABRICS USED

- **Charm Packs:** *Canning Day by Corey Yoder for Moda Fabrics*
- **Fabric A:** *Bella Solids in White by Moda Fabrics*
- **Background fabric:** *Bella Solids in Dark Teal by Moda Fabrics*

The alternate colorway of the *Carnegie Plaid* quilt was quilted with a loopy design.

Snapdragon Cove

Pieced and quilted by
Cheryl Brickey

finished block

8″ × 8″

finished quilt

56½″ × 64½″

social media

#SnapdragonCoveQuilt

THIS DESIGN REMINDS ME of columns of intersecting diamonds and uses my favorite block,
half-square triangles.

Fabric Requirements

Width of fabrics (WOF) is assumed to be at least 40˝.

CHARM SQUARES 5˝ × 5˝: 80

FABRIC A (WHITE): ⅞ yard

BACKGROUND (BG) FABRIC (TEAL): 2 yards

BINDING: ⅝ yard

BACKING FABRIC: 3⅔ yards

BATTING: 65˝ × 73˝

Cutting Instructions

CHARM SQUARES

The charm squares 5˝ × 5˝ will be used without further cutting.

FABRIC A (WHITE)

- Cut 5 strips 5˝ × WOF.

   a. Sub-cut the strips into 40 squares 5˝ × 5˝ (each strip can yield 8 squares).

BACKGROUND (BG) FABRIC (TEAL)

- Cut 7 strips 5˝ × WOF.

   a. Sub-cut the strips into 56 squares 5˝ × 5˝ (each strip can yield 8 squares).

- Cut 6 strips 4½˝ × WOF.

   a. Sub-cut 2 strips into 8 rectangles 4½˝ × 8½˝ (each strip can yield 4 rectangles).

   b. Reserve the remaining 4 strips for the border.

BINDING FABRIC

Cut 7 strips 2½˝ × WOF.

Piecing Instructions

A scant ¼˝ (a thread width smaller than ¼˝) seam is to be used throughout the construction of the quilt top unless otherwise instructed.

Half-Square Triangle (HST) Units

1. Place a charm square 5˝ × 5˝ and a fabric A square 5˝ × 5˝ right sides together. Draw a diagonal line using a removable marking device on the back of the lighter square (shown as the solid line).

2. Sew a ¼˝ seam on both sides of the solid line (shown as the dotted lines). Cut on the solid line and press seam open or towards the darker fabric.

3. Trim the charm/A HST units to 4½˝ × 4½˝. Note: each set of one charm square and one fabric A square will yield two HST units.

4. Repeat steps 1–3 to make a total of 64 charm/A HST units 4½˝ × 4½˝.

5. Repeat steps 1–3 using charm squares and bg squares 5˝ × 5˝ to make a total of 96 charm/bg HST units 4½˝ × 4½˝.

6. Repeat steps 1–3 using fabric A squares 5˝ × 5˝ and bg squares 5˝ × 5˝ to make a total of 16 A/bg HST units 4½˝ × 4½˝.

- **Charm Packs:** *Indigo Garden by Heather Peterson for Riley Blake Fabrics*

- **Fabric A:** *Confetti Cotton Solids in Riley White by Riley Blake*

- **Background fabric:** *Confetti Cotton Solids in Cape Verde by Riley Blake*

Block A

1. Sew together 4 charm/bg HST blocks 4½˝ × 4½˝, pressing the seams open, to make a block A 8½˝ × 8½˝.

2. Repeat to make a total of 17 block A.

Block B

1. Sew together 4 charm/A HST blocks 4½˝ × 4½˝, pressing the seams open, to make a block B 8½˝ × 8½˝.

2. Repeat to make a total of 10 block B.

Block C

1. Sew together 2 charm/A HST blocks 4½˝ × 4½˝ and 2 charm/bg HST blocks 4½˝ × 4½˝, pressing the seams open, to make a block C 8½˝ × 8½˝.

2. Repeat to make a total of 8 block C.

Block D

1. Sew together 2 A/bg HST blocks 4½˝ × 4½˝, pressing the seam open, to make a block D 4½˝ × 8½˝.

2. Repeat to make a total of 6 block D.

Quilt Top Assembly

First Rows

1. Sew together the following blocks and pieces, pressing the seams open, to make a first row 8½˝ × 48½˝.

2 block A 8½˝ × 8½˝

1 block B 8½˝ × 8½˝

2 block C 8½˝ × 8½˝

2 bg rectangles 4½˝ × 8½˝

2. Repeat to make a total of 4 first rows.

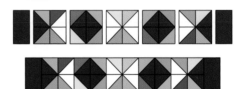

Second Rows

1. Sew together the following blocks, pressing the seams open, to make a second row 8½˝ × 48½˝.

3 block A 8½˝ × 8½˝

2 block B 8½˝ × 8½˝

2 block D 4½˝ × 8½˝

2. Repeat to make a total of 3 second rows.

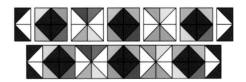

Third Rows

1. Sew together the following units, pressing the seams open, to make a third row 4½″ × 48½″.

4 charm/A HST units 4½″ × 4½″

6 charm/bg HST units 4½″ × 4½″

2 A/bg HST units 4½″ × 4½″

Be sure to match the direction of all of the HST units.

2. Repeat to make a total of 2 third rows.

Quilt Top Assembly

1. Sew together the following rows as shown in the quilt top assembly diagram, pressing the seams open, to make the quilt top.

4 first rows 8½″ × 48½″

3 second rows 8½″ × 48½″

2 third rows 4½″ × 48½″

The quilt top, before the borders are added, should measure 48½″ × 64½″.

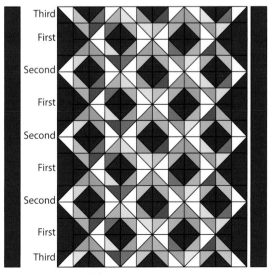

Quilt Top Assembly Diagram

Border

Refer to the quilt top assembly diagram.

1. Sew together 2 bg strips 4½″ × WOF and trim to the average height of the quilt, approx. 64½″. Repeat to make a second side border.

2. Sew side borders onto the quilt top, pressing seams open or towards the borders.

The finished quilt top should measure approx. 56½″ × 64½″.

Finishing

Refer to Finishing the Quilt (page 124) for instructions on how to finish the quilt.

1. Make the quilt backing:

Remove selvages, cut into 2 pieces (about 65″ × WOF) and sew backing pieces together along the trimmed selvage edges using a ½″ seam, pressing the seam open. Trim to approx. 65″ × 73″.

2. Layer the quilt top, batting, and backing. Baste and quilt as desired.

The main colorway of the *Snapdragon Cove* quilt was quilted with back and forth and stipple designs.

3. Trim off selvages from the binding strips 2½″ × WOF and sew together end-to-end to make the binding. Bind and enjoy your quilt!

alternate colorway

Pieced and quilted by Cheryl Brickey

FABRICS USED

- **Charm Packs:** *Strawberry & Friends by Kimberly Kight for Ruby Star Society*
- **Fabric A:** *Bella Solids in White by Moda Fabrics*
- **Background fabric:** *Bella Solids in Steel by Moda Fabrics*

The alternate colorway of the *Snapdragon Cove* quilt was quilted with a looping design.

String Lights

Pieced by Cheryl Brickey and quilted by the Bear Creek Quilting Company

finished quilt

57½″ × 67″

social media

#StringLightsQuilt

AS SOON AS I DESIGNED this quilt, my son looked at it and said that it looked like the string lights his sister has hanging in her room, so that is how this quilt earned its name.

Fabric Requirements

Width of fabrics (WOF) is assumed to be at least 40˝.

CHARM SQUARES 5˝ × 5˝: 71

FABRIC A (GOLD): ⅜ yard

BACKGROUND (BG) FABRIC (BLACK): 3⅜ yards

BINDING: ⅝ yard

BACKING FABRIC: 3⅔ yards

BATTING: 66˝ × 75˝

Cutting Instructions

CHARM SQUARES

- Trim 47 charm squares to 4˝ × 4˝.

- The remaining 24 charm squares 5˝ × 5˝ will be used without further cutting.

FABRIC A (GOLD)

- Cut 1 strip 5˝ × WOF.

  a. Sub-cut the strip into 4 squares 5˝ × 5˝.

- Cut 1 strip 4˝ × WOF.

  a. Sub-cut the strip into 8 squares 4˝ × 4˝.

BACKGROUND (BG) FABRIC (BLACK)

- Cut 4 strips 5˝ × WOF.

  a. Sub-cut the strips into 28 squares 5˝ × 5˝ (each strip can yield 8 squares).

- Cut 5 strips 4½˝ × WOF.

  a. Sub-cut 1 strip into 4 squares 4½˝ × 4½˝.

  b. Reserve the remaining 4 strips.

- Cut 4 strips 4˝ × WOF.

  a. Sub-cut 1 strip to 1 rectangle 4˝ × 39˝.

  b. Sub-cut 1 strip to 1 rectangle 4˝ × 32˝.

  c. Sub-cut 1 strip into 1 rectangle 4˝ × 28½˝ and 1 rectangle 4˝ × 11˝.

  d. Sub-cut 1 strip into 1 rectangle 4˝ × 14½˝, 1 rectangle 4˝ × 7½˝, and 1 square 4˝ × 4˝.

- Cut 14 strips 3½˝ × WOF.

BINDING FABRIC

Cut 7 strips 2½˝ × WOF.

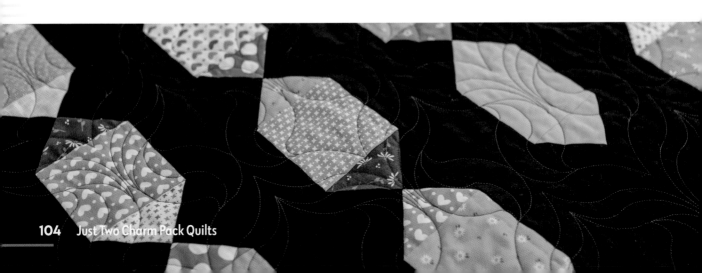

FABRICS USED

- **Charm Packs:** *Sincerely Yours by Sherri & Chelsi for Moda Fabrics*
- **Fabric A:** *Bella Solids in Sunflower by Moda Fabrics*
- **Background fabric:** *Bella Solids in Black by Moda Fabrics*

Piecing Instructions

A scant ¼˝ (a thread width smaller than ¼˝) seam is to be used throughout the construction of the quilt top unless otherwise instructed.

Half-Square Triangle (HST) Units

1. Place a charm square 5˝ × 5˝ and a bg square 5˝ × 5˝ right sides together. Draw a diagonal line using a removable marking device on the back of the lighter square (shown as the solid line).

2. Sew a ¼˝ seam on both sides of the solid line (shown as the dotted lines). Cut on the solid line and press seam open or towards the darker fabric to make a charm/bg HST unit. *Do not trim these HST units.*

3. Repeat steps 1–2 to make a total of 48 charm/bg HST units about 4½˝ × 4½˝.

4. Repeat steps 1–2 using fabric A squares 5˝ × 5˝ and bg squares 5˝ × 5˝ to make a total of 8 A/bg HST units about 4½˝ × 4½˝. *Do not trim these HST units.*

Full Hourglass Units

1. Place 2 charm/bg HST units about 4½˝ × 4½˝ right sides together such that the seams nest together and HST units are oriented as shown in the illustration.

2. Draw a diagonal line using a removable marking device on the back of the one of the HST units (shown as the solid line) perpendicular to the seam of that HST unit.

3. Sew a ¼˝ seam on each side of the solid line (shown as the dotted lines). Cut on the solid line, press seams open, and trim charm/ bg hourglass units to 4˝ × 4˝.

4. Repeat steps 1–3 to make a total of 44 charm/charm full hourglass units 4˝ × 4˝ (43 will be used in the quilt top).

5. Repeat steps 1–3 using charm/bg HST units about 4½˝ × 4½˝ and fabric A/bg HST units 4½˝ × 4½˝ to make a total of 8 charm/A full hourglass units 4½˝ × 4½˝.

Partial Hourglass Units

1. Place 1 fabric A/bg HST unit about 4½″ × 4½″ and 1 bg square 4½″ × 4½″ right sides together.

2. Draw a diagonal line using a removable marking device on the back of the fabric A/bg HST unit (shown as the solid line) perpendicular to the seam of that HST unit.

3. Sew a ¼″ seam on each side of the solid line (shown as the dotted lines). Cut on the solid line, press seams open, and trim the partial hourglass units to 4″ × 4″.

Note that the seam orientation in the bg area does not matter.

4. Repeat steps 1–3 to make a total of 8 partial hourglass units 4″ × 4″.

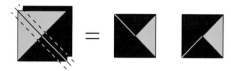

Quilt Top Assembly

It is recommended that all seams are pressed open or away from the full and partial hourglass units during the quilt top assembly.

Block Columns

Follow the chart and block column assemblies illustration (page 108) to make the 8 block columns, each measuring 4″ × 67″.

	# of charm squares 4″ × 4″	# of charm hourglass units 4″ × 4″	# of charm/fabric A hourglass units 4″ × 4″	# of partial hourglass units 4″ × 4″	Fabric A squares 4″ × 4″	Additional bg pieces
Col 1	7	7	1	1	1	4″ × 7½″
Col 2	4	3	1	1	1	4″ × 32″
Col 3	6	6	1	1	1	4″ × 14½″
Col 4	3	2	1	1	1	4″ × 39″
Col 5	8	8	1	1	1	none
Col 6	7	6	1	1	1	4″ × 11″
Col 7	4	4	1	1	1	4″ × 28½″
Col 8	8	7	1	1	1	4″ × 4″

Inner Sashing Columns

1. Sew together 2 bg strips 3½″ × WOF and trim to the average height of the quilt, approx. 67″.

2. Repeat to make a total of 7 inner sashing columns 3½″ × 67″.

Outer Sashing Columns

1. Sew together 2 bg strips 4½″ × WOF and trim to the average height of the quilt, approx. 67″.

2. Repeat to make a total of 2 outer sashing columns 4½″ × 67″.

Quilt Top Assembly

Sew together the following columns as shown in the quilt top assembly diagram, pressing the seams open or towards the sashing columns, to make the quilt top, approx. 57½″ × 67″.

8 block columns 4″ × 67″

7 inner sashing columns 3½″ × 67″

2 outer sashing columns 4½″ × 67″

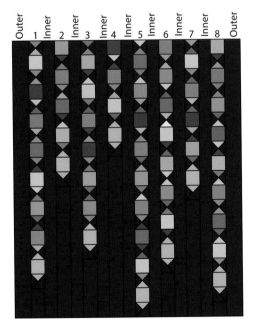

Block Col 1

Block Col 2

Block Col 3

Block Col 4

Block Col 5

Block Col 6

Block Col 7

Block Col 8

Block Column Assemblies

Finishing

Refer to Finishing the Quilt (page 124) for instructions on how to finish the quilt.

1. Make the quilt backing:

Remove selvages, cut into 2 pieces (about 66″ × WOF) and sew backing pieces together along the trimmed selvage edges using a ½″ seam, pressing the seam open. Trim to approx. 66″ × 75″.

2. Layer the quilt top, batting, and backing. Baste and quilt as desired. The main colorway of the *String Lights* quilt was quilted with a vertical scroll design.

3. Trim off selvages from the binding strips 2½″ × WOF and sew together end-to-end to make the binding. Bind and enjoy your quilt!

Quilt Top Assembly Diagram

alternate colorway

Pieced and quilted by Delia Dorn

FABRICS USED

- **Charm Packs:** *Peppermint by Dana Willard for FIGO Fabrics*
- **Fabric A:** *Colorworks Solids in Superwhite by Northcott Fabrics*
- **Background fabric:** *Colorworks Solids in Bubblegum by Northcott Fabrics*

The alternate colorway of the *String Lights* quilt was quilted with a custom holly leave and ball design, complementing the main charm print of the collection.

Abby & Katie

Pieced and Quilted by
Michele Blake

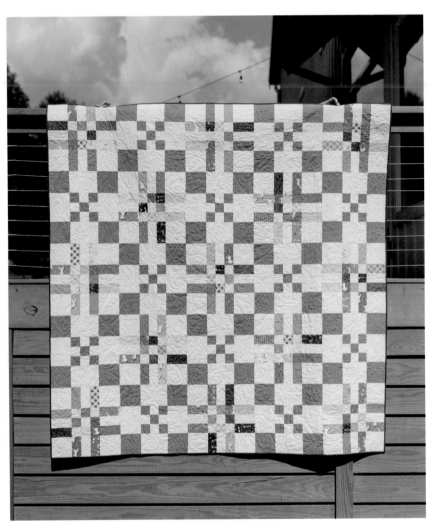

finished block
15″ × 15″

finished quilt
75½″ × 75½″

social media
#AbbyAndKatieQuilt

THIS QUILT is built from two alternating blocks and is named after my two pets that have passed away, Abby the cat and Katie the dog.

FABRICS USED

- **Charm Packs:** *Meander by Aneela Hoey for Moda Fabrics*
- **Fabric A:** *Bella Solids in Etchings Slate by Moda Fabrics*
- **Background fabric:** *Bella Solids in Feather by Moda Fabrics*

Fabric Requirements

Width of fabrics (WOF) is assumed to be at least 40˝.

CHARM SQUARES 5˝ × 5˝: 78

FABRIC A (GRAY): 1⅜ yards

BACKGROUND (BG) FABRIC (WHITE): 3¼ yards

BINDING: ¾ yard

BACKING FABRIC: 7 yards

BATTING: 84˝ × 84˝

Cutting Instructions

CHARM SQUARES

- Cut 13 charm squares each in half horizontally and vertically to make a total of 52 squares 2½˝ × 2½˝.

- The remaining 65 charm squares 5˝ × 5˝ will be used without further cutting.

FABRIC A (GRAY)

- Cut 6 strips 5˝ × WOF.

  a. Sub-cut the strips into 48 squares 5˝ × 5˝ (each strip can yield 8 squares).

- Cut 5 strips 2½˝ × WOF.

BACKGROUND (BG) FABRIC (WHITE)

- Cut 15 strips 5˝ × WOF.

  a. Sub-cut 8 strips into 48 rectangles 5˝ × 6½˝ (each strip can yield 6 rectangles).

  b. Sub-cut 7 strips into 52 squares 5˝ × 5˝ (each strip can yield 8 squares).

- Cut 12 strips 2½˝ × WOF.

  a. Sub-cut 7 strips into 52 rectangles 2½˝ × 5˝ (each strip can yield 8 rectangles).

  b. Sub-cut 1 strip into 13 squares 2½˝ × 2½˝.

  c. Reserve the remaining 4 strips.

BINDING FABRIC

Cut 8 strips 2½˝ × WOF.

Piecing Instructions

A scant ¼˝ (a thread width smaller than ¼˝) seam is to be used throughout the construction of the quilt top unless otherwise instructed.

Block A

1. Sew together the following pieces, pressing the seam open or away from the charm square, to make an insert unit 2½˝ × 7˝.

- 1 charm square 2½˝ × 2½˝
- 1 bg rectangle 2½˝ × 5˝

2. Repeat to make a total of 52 insert units.

3. Sew together the following pieces, pressing the seams open or as shown, to make an intermediate unit 14˝ × 14˝.

- 5 charm squares 5˝ × 5˝
- 4 bg rectangles 5˝ × 5˝

4. Repeat to make a total of 13 intermediate units.

5. Cut each intermediate unit 14″ × 14″ in half vertically and horizontally to make a total of 52 quarter units 7″ × 7″. The cut should measure 7″ from each side (2¼″ from the inner seams).

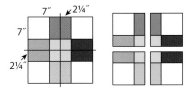

6. Using units having a variety of charm prints, sew together the following units and pieces, pressing the seams open, to make a block A 15½″ × 15½″ (15″ × 15″ finished in the quilt top).

    4 quarter units 7″ × 7″

    4 inset units 2½″ × 7″

    1 bg square 2½″ × 2½″

7. Repeat to make a total of 13 block A. *If your seams were pressed to the side, there may be a few seams within the middle of the block A that do not nest.*

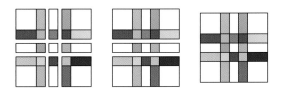

Block B

1. Sew together 2 fabric A strips 2½″ × WOF and 1 bg strip 2½″ × WOF, pressing the seams open or towards the darker fabric, to make a first strip set 6½″ × WOF.

2. Repeat to make a total of 2 first strip sets.

3. Cut the first strip sets into 24 first segments 2½″ × 6½″ (each strip set can yield 16 segments).

4. Sew together 1 fabric A strip 2½″ × WOF and 2 bg strips 2½″ × WOF, pressing the seams open or towards the darker fabric, to make a second strip set 6½″ × WOF.

5. Cut the second strip set into 12 second segments 2½″ × 6½″.

6. Sew together the following segments, pressing the seams open, to make a center unit 6½″ × 6½″.

    2 first strip set segments

    1 second strip set segment

7. Repeat to make a total of 12 center units.

8. Sew together the following units and pieces, pressing the seams open or as shown by the arrows to make a block B 15½″ × 15½″ (15″ × 15″ finished in the quilt top).

    1 center unit 6½″ × 6½″

    4 fabric A squares 5″ × 5″

    4 bg rectangles 5″ × 6½″

9. Repeat to make a total of 12 block B.

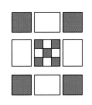 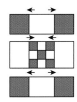

Quilt Top Assembly

First Rows

1. Sew together the following blocks, pressing the seams open or towards block B, to make a first row 15½˝ × 75½˝.

  3 block A 15½˝ × 15½˝

  2 block B 15½˝ × 15½˝

2. Repeat to make a total of 3 first rows.

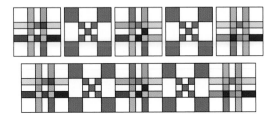

Second Rows

1. Sew together the following blocks, pressing the seams open or towards block B, to make a second row 15½˝ × 75½˝.

  2 block A 15½˝ × 15½˝

  3 block B 15½˝ × 15½˝

2. Repeat to make a total of 2 second rows.

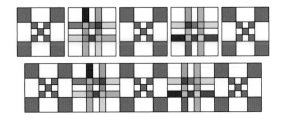

Quilt Top Assembly

Referring to the quilt top assembly diagram, sew the following rows together, pressing the seams open, to make the quilt top approx. 75½˝ × 75½˝.

  3 first rows 15½˝ × 75½˝

  2 second rows 15½˝ × 75½˝

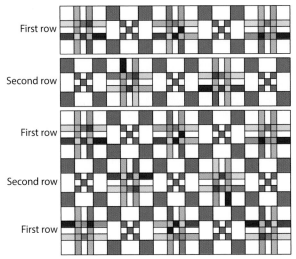

Quilt Top Assembly Diagram

Finishing

Refer to Finishing the Quilt (page 124) for instructions on how to finish the quilt.

1. Make the quilt backing:

Remove selvages, cut into 3 pieces (about 84˝ × WOF) and sew backing pieces together along the trimmed selvage edges using a ½˝ seam, pressing the seam open. Trim to approx. 84˝ × 84˝.

2. Layer the quilt top, batting, and backing. Baste and quilt as desired. The main colorway of the *Abby & Katie* quilt was quilted with a Swirl Hook design.

3. Trim off selvages from the binding strips 2½˝ × WOF and sew together end-to-end to make the binding. Bind and enjoy your quilt!

alternate colorway

FABRICS USED

- **Charm Packs:** *Sun Print Luminance by Alison Glass for Andover Fabrics*
- **Fabric A:** *Century Solids in Raspberry by Andover Fabrics*
- **Background fabric:** *Century Solids in Sky by Andover Fabrics*

The alternate colorway of the *Abby & Katie* quilt was quilted with a Spiral Swirl design.

Diamond Hashtag

Pieced by Paige Taylor and quilted by Valorie Kasten

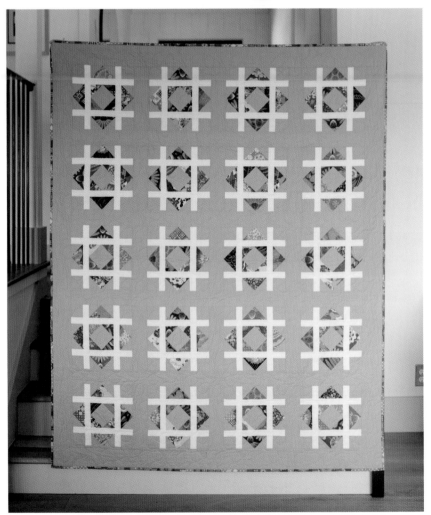

finished block

10″ × 10″

finished quilt

55″ × 67½″

social media

#DiamondHashtagQuilt

DIAMOND HASHTAG combines a diamond block and a tic toe board for an interesting block design.

FABRICS USED

- **Charm Packs:** *Love Always by Anna Maria Horner for FreeSpirit Fabrics*
- **Fabric A:** *Essential Solids in White by FreeSpirit Fabrics*
- **Background fabric:** *Essential Solids in Oasis by FreeSpirit Fabrics*

Fabric Requirements

Width of fabrics (WOF) is assumed to be at least 40˝.

CHARM SQUARES 5˝ × 5˝: 80

FABRIC A (WHITE): 1¼ yards

BACKGROUND (BG) FABRIC (LIGHT GREEN): 3 yards

BINDING: ⅝ yard

BACKING FABRIC: 3½ yards

BATTING: 63˝ × 76˝

Cutting Instructions

CHARM SQUARES

Cut 40 charm squares each into 2 rectangles 2½˝ × 4½˝.

Trim remaining 40 charm squares each to 3˝ × 3˝.

Tip If you like to oversize your triangles for square in a square blocks, you can trim the charm squares to 3½˝ × 3½˝.

FABRIC A (WHITE)

- Cut 24 strips 1½˝ × WOF.

  a. Sub-cut 14 strips into 40 rectangles 1½˝ × 10½˝ (each strip can yield 3 rectangles).

  Note: if your WOF is at least 42˝, then each strip can yield 4 rectangles and only 10 strips are needed.

  b. Sub-cut 5 strips into 40 rectangles 1½˝ × 4½˝ (each strip can yield 8 rectangles).

  c. Sub-cut 5 strips into 80 rectangles 1½˝ × 2½˝ (each strip can yield 16 rectangles).

BACKGROUND (BG) FABRIC (LIGHT GREEN)

- Cut 6 strips 4˝ × WOF for the border.

- Cut 10 strips 3˝ × WOF.

  a. Sub-cut 5 strips into 15 rectangles 3˝ × 10½˝ (each strip can yield 3 rectangles).

  Note: if your WOF is at least 42˝, then each strip can yield 4 rectangles and only 4 strips are needed.

  b. Reserve the remaining 5 strips.

- Cut 2 strips 3⅜˝ × WOF.

  a. Sub-cut the strips into 20 squares 3⅜˝ × 3⅜˝ (each strip can yield 11 squares).

- Cut 15 strips 2½˝ × WOF.

  a. Sub-cut the strips into 240 squares 2½˝ × 2½˝ (each strip can yield 16 squares).

BINDING FABRIC

Cut 7 strips 2½˝ × WOF.

Piecing Instructions

A scant ¼˝ (a thread width smaller than ¼˝) seam is to be used throughout the construction of the quilt top unless otherwise instructed.

Flying Geese Units

1. Place a bg square 2½˝ × 2½˝ on one side of a charm rectangle 2½˝ × 4½˝ right sides together.

Draw a diagonal line on the back of the bg square using a removable marking device and sew on the marked line (shown as the dotted line).

Trim a ¼˝ from the stitched line and press seam towards the bg fabric.

2. Place a bg square 2½˝ × 2½˝ on the opposite end of the charm rectangle and sew together as in step 1.

3. Trim flying geese unit to 2½˝ × 4½˝ if necessary, making sure there is ¼˝ between the point of the charm triangle and the edge of the flying geese unit.

4. Repeat steps 1–3 to make a total of 80 flying geese units 2½˝ × 4½˝.

Square in a Square Units

Use a variety of prints within each square in a square unit.

1. Cut each of the charm squares 3˝ × 3˝ (or 3½˝ × 3½˝ if you oversized them) in half once on the diagonal.

2. Center a charm triangle 3˝ × 3˝ along a first side of a bg square 3⅜˝ × 3⅜˝. Sew along the edge with a scant ¼˝ seam (shown as a dotted line), pressing seam open or outwards.

3. Sew a second charm triangle 3˝ × 3˝ on the side of the bg square opposite to the first side, pressing seam open or outwards. *Note: you can sew both of these triangles on then press instead of pressing after each addition.*

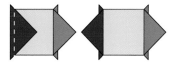

4. Continue by sewing 2 charm triangles 3″ × 3″ onto the other 2 sides of the square, pressing seams open or outwards.

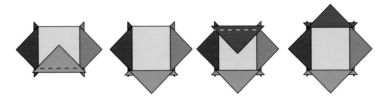

5. Trim off the tabs (dog ears) formed by the sewn-on triangles and square the unit to 4½″ × 4½″ (if necessary) making sure there is ¼″ between the corner of the inner square and the outer side of the unit.

6. Repeat steps 2–5 to make a total of 20 square in a square units.

Outer Block Rows

1. Sew together the following units and pieces, pressing the seams open or towards the fabric A pieces, to make an outer block row 2½″ × 10½″.

    1 flying geese unit 2½″ × 4½″

    2 fabric A rectangles 1½″ × 2½″

    2 bg squares 2½″ × 2½″

2. Repeat to make a total of 40 outer block rows.

Inner Block Rows

1. Sew together the following units and pieces, pressing the seams open or towards the fabric A pieces, to make an inner block row 4½″ × 10½″.

    1 square in a square unit 4½″ × 4½″

    2 flying geese units 2½″ × 4½″

    2 fabric A rectangles 1½″ × 4½″

2. Repeat to make a total of 20 inner block rows.

Block Assembly

1. Sew together the following rows, pressing the seams open or towards fabric A, to make a block 10½″ × 10½″.

    1 inner block row 4½″ × 10½″

    2 outer block rows 2½″ × 10½″

    2 fabric A rectangles 1½″ × 10½″

2. Repeat to make a total of 20 blocks.

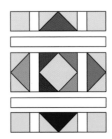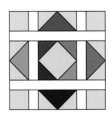

Quilt Top Assembly

Block Rows

1. Sew together the following blocks and pieces, pressing the seams open or towards the bg rectangles, to make a block row 10½″ × 48″.

> 4 blocks 10½″ × 10½″

> 3 bg rectangles 3″ × 10½″

2. Repeat to make a total of 5 block rows.

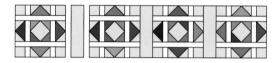

Sashing Rows

Cut 1 bg strip 3″ × WOF into fourths (each 3″ by approx. 10″) and sew each fourth to a full bg strip 3″ × WOF to make a total of 4 sashing rows. Trim each sashing row to the average width of the quilt, approx. 48″.

Quilt Top Assembly

Sew together the following rows as shown in the quilt top assembly diagram, pressing the seams open or towards the sashing rows, to make the quilt top.

> 5 block rows 10½″ × 48″

> 4 sashing rows 3″ × 48″

The quilt top, before borders are added, should measure 48″ × 60½″.

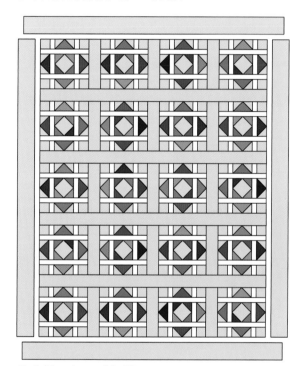

Quilt Top Assembly Diagram

Border

Refer to the quilt top assembly diagram.

1. Cut 1 bg strip 4″ × WOF in half and sew each half to a full bg strip 4″ × WOF. Trim to the average height of the quilt, approx. 60½″. *Note: if your strips are not 60½″, trim an inch or two off of another 4″ × WOF and sew it onto the strips.*

2. Sew borders onto the sides of the quilt top, pressing the seams open or towards the borders.

3. Cut 1 bg strip 4″ × WOF in half and sew each half to a full bg strip 4″ × WOF. Trim to the average width of the quilt, approx. 55″.

4. Sew borders onto the top and bottom of the quilt top, pressing seams open or towards the borders.

The finished quilt top should measure approx. 55″ × 67½″.

Finishing

Refer to Finishing the Quilt (page 124) for instructions on how to finish the quilt.

1. Make the quilt backing:

Remove selvages, cut into 2 pieces (about 63″ × WOF) and sew backing pieces together along the trimmed selvage edges using a ½″ seam, pressing the seam open. Trim to approx. 63″ × 76″.

2. Layer the quilt top, batting, and backing. Baste and quilt as desired. The main colorway of the *Diamond Hashtag* quilt was quilted with a leaf design.

3. Trim off selvages from the binding strips 2½″ × WOF and sew together end-to-end to make the binding. Bind and enjoy your quilt!

FABRICS USED

- **Charm Packs:** *Sonnet Dusk by Corri Sheff for Riley Blake Fabrics*
- **Fabric A:** *Confetti Cotton Solids in Charcoal by Riley Blake Fabrics*
- **Background fabric:** *Confetti Cotton Solids in White by Riley Blake Fabrics*

The alternate colorway of the *Diamond Hashtag* quilt was quilted with a modern baptist fan design.

Finishing the Quilt

Making the Quilt Sandwich

1. Lay the backing wrong side up and tape the edges down with masking tape. If you are working on carpet you can use T-pins to secure the backing to the carpet.

2. Center the batting on top of the backing, smoothing out any folds and creases.

3. Place the quilt top, right side up, on top of the batting, making sure it is centered on the batting.

Basting

Basting keeps the quilt sandwich layers from shifting while quilting.

One basting option is to use a temporary spray adhesive between the backing/batting and the batting/quilt top. Be sure to follow the manufacturer's directions, use in a well-ventilated area, and protect the surrounding area from overspray.

Another option for basting is pin basting. Pin the quilt layers together with safety pins placed about 3″ to 4″ apart. Begin basting in the center and move toward the edges.

Other basting options include basting by hand with thread or having a longarm quilter baste the quilt.

Quilting

Quilting, whether by machine or hand, serves to attach all three layers of the quilt sandwich together and can enhance the design of the quilt. The 32 quilts in this book showcase many different quilting designs from walking foot quilting to free motion quilting to professional longarm quilting.

Binding

The first step in binding is to square up the quilt. Squaring up is the process of trimming the excess batting and backing off the quilted quilt and making sure each of the corners of the quilt are square (90 degrees). To prepare for binding, trim excess batting and backing from the quilt even with the edges of the quilt top, squaring up if necessary.

Making the Binding

tip STRAIGHT GRAIN VERSUS BIAS GRAIN BINDING The instructions and fabric requirements for the quilts in this book are for straight grain binding, meaning that the strips for the binding are cut from selvedge to selvage. Some quilters prefer a bias binding where the strips are cut at a 45 degree angle to the selvedges. If bias binding is your preferred method for binding, additional binding fabric may be required compared to what is listed in the pattern.

Cut the binding strips crosswise (from selvedge to selvedge) and piece them together with diagonal seams to make a continuous binding strip. Trim the seam allowances to ¼″ and press the seams open.

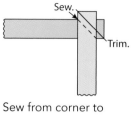

Sew from corner to corner.

Completed diagonal seam

Press the entire strip in half lengthwise with wrong sides together.

Attaching the Binding

Pin the binding to the front edge of one side of the quilt, away from the corner (raw edges of the binding and quilt top aligned) along one side of the quilt and leave the first 8″-10″ inches of the binding unattached. Start sewing the binding onto the quilt top, using a ¼″ seam allowance.

1. Stop ¼″ away from the first corner, back stitch, and cut the thread. Rotate the quilt one-quarter turn.

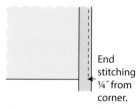

End stitching ¼″ from corner.

Stitch and stop ¼″ from corner.

Fold the binding at a right angle so it extends straight above the quilt and the fold forms a 45° angle in the corner.

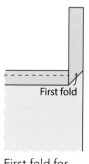

First fold

First fold for miter

Bring the binding strip down even with the edge of the quilt and begin sewing the next side of the quilt from the folded edge. Repeat for all of the corners.

Second fold

Second fold alignment

Continue stitching until 10″ to 12″ from where the binding was first sewn down to the quilt. Overlap the binding ends and at a point near the middle of the gap between the starting and stopping points. Cut the binding tails so that they overlap 2½″ (the width of the binding strip).

Open both binding ends and place one end on top of the other end at right angles, right sides together. Mark a diagonal line from corner to corner and stitch on the line. Check that the binding fits the quilt; then trim the seam allowance to ¼″. Finger press the seam open.

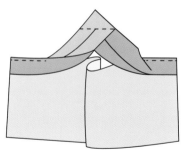

Stitch ends of binding diagonally.

Stitch this last binding section in place on the quilt. Fold the binding over to the quilt back and hand stitch in place mitering the corners. Alternatively, the binding can be sewn to the back of the quilt using the sewing machine.

About the Author ■

CHERYL BRICKEY began quilting in 2010 to make her then toddler daughter a quilt for her first bed and has been quilting non-stop since. She was born and raised in New Jersey and now calls South Carolina home, where she and her husband are raising their two children. Cheryl has a chemical engineering degree from Carnegie Mellon University and spends her days writing patent applications for a private textile and chemical company. She combines her technical writing, engineering, and math skills in each of her quilt designs, with quilt math being one of her favorite elements to pattern writing.

Photograph by Melissa Dorn

Cheryl is an active member of the Greenville Modern Quilt Guild and is also very involved with the online quilting community. She has taught modern quilt design, sewing and quilting techniques, and computer aided quilt design across the country to guilds and at national quilt shows.

Cheryl has won numerous awards for her quilts and designs and has been featured on the Moda Bake Shop, in *Modern Quilts Unlimited*, *Quiltmaker*, *Modern Patchwork*, *Make Modern*, and *Quilty*, and in QuiltCon and other international quilt shows.

Cheryl's first book *Modern Plus Sign Quilts* (Stash 2018), co-authored with Paige Alexander, explored her love of the traditional plus sign block and her second book *Just One Charm Pack Quilts* (Stash 2021) helps quilters use their stash with quilts using only one charm pack.

You can find more of Cheryl's work on her website **MeadowMistDesigns.com** and on Instagram **@MeadowMistDesigns**.

About the Quilter

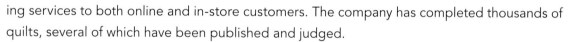SHARI SHOBE is a passionate creator, born and raised in the Pacific Northwest. Her love of nature and wildlife inspires her creativity both personally and professionally.

Shari has become an industry expert and a trend setter inspiring quilters around the world. She has designed and published patterns, written articles, and sewn over 100 quilts. Shari also owns and operates Bear Creek Quilting Company. Additionally she has worked with a multitude of other types of crafts.

Bear Creek Quilting Company offers a growing variety of products and longarm quilting services to both online and in-store customers. The company has completed thousands of quilts, several of which have been published and judged.

When she is away from her quilt shop Shari can be found creating in her sewing studio, enjoying outdoor gardening and bird watching. Shari and the Bear Creek Quilting Company longarm quilted many of the quilts in this book.

CREATIVE SpARK
ONLINE LEARNING

Crafty courses to become an expert maker...

From their studio to yours, Creative Spark instructors are teaching you how to create and become a master of your craft. So not only do you get a look inside their creative space, you also get to be a part of engaging courses that would typically be a one or multi-day workshop from the comfort of your home.

Creative Spark is not your one-size-fits-all online learning experience. We welcome you to be who you are, share, create, and belong.

Scan for a gift from

creativespark.ctpub.com